I0475653

Replacement Bellows
for Folding Cameras

Daniel R. Mitchell

Replacement Bellows for Folding Cameras
By Daniel R. Mitchell

Copyright 2007 Daniel R. Mitchell, All Rights Reserved

Published by Daniel Mitchell (http://daniel.mitchell.name)

ISBN 978-1-304-52146-0

Table of Contents

Introduction 5
Overview...8
   Parallel and Tapered Shapes 8
   Bellows Construction...9
Bellows Dimensions 11
   Variable Taper 12
   Bellows Length 13
   Bellows Width...15
   Folds 16
   Number of folds and Thickness of Material.........17
Understanding Bellows Folds 18
   Triangular Folds 18
   Square Corners 19
   Fold Ribs and Gaps 19
   Alternating Widths on a Tapered Bellows 20
   Stiffener Rib Shape 23
   Practice Tapered Bellows......................................24
Frame Attachment 25
   Octagonal Front Frame...25
   Rectangular Front Frame 27
   Rear Attachment Through the Camera Body.........29
   Rear Attachment In Front of Camera Body 30
Seams...31
Tools..33
   Basic Camera Tools 33
   Knife and/or scissors and cutting mat 34
   Ruler and Square 34
   Clamps 35
   Solvents and Lubricants 35
Bellows Materials...36
   Total thickness..36
   Liner Cloth 36
   Covering 38
   Stiffener Ribs 39
   Adhesives...39
Steps in Making a Bellows 41
Removing the Old Bellows..42
Measuring Bellows Dimensions...................................45
   Bellows Length 45

Bellows Width..45
Bellows Folds...46
Drawing The Patterns 48
Templates 48
Complete pattern...50
Stiffener Rib Pattern 51
Making a Form 55
Assembly of the New Bellows 56
Installing the Bellows..58
Sample Bellows Patterns 60
6x6 Top/Bottom (Generic)...61
6x6 Sides (Generic) 62
6x9 Top/Bottom (Wirgin Presto) 63
6x9 Sides (Wirgin Presto)...64
6x9 Sides (Wirgin Auta)..65
6x9 Top/Bottom (Wirgin Auta) 66
6x9 Sides (Billy Record) 67
6x9 Top/Bottom (Billy Record) 68
6x9 Sides (No. 1 Kodak Autographic Special) 69
6x9 Top/Bottom (No. 1 Kodak Autographic Special) 70

Introduction

For the first half of the 20th century one of the most popular camera types for amateur use was the small folding bellows camera. Early folding cameras used small plates and were similar in operation to view cameras. Later, folding cameras began to use various sizes of roll film instead of sheet films. Like a box camera, the roll film folders could take several pictures without having to carry around plate holders and sheets of film. Unlike a box camera, the folders would collapse down to a thin size and could be easily carried in a coat pocket, purse or briefcase. Folding cameras remained very popular until displaced by 35mm cameras. Consequently, there are a large number of these types of cameras available to collectors and amateur photographers today.

Folding cameras range in specification from very simple cameras with an I/B/T box camera shutter and fixed focus meniscus lens to professional quality cameras with fast four element lenses, full range of shutter speeds, and built in range finder. In between there exist a wide variety of cameras with good quality triplet lens and a wide range of shutter speeds. The larger negative size of the roll film formats will produce high quality images even with a lower specification lens. In many cases, these are still very good cameras to use for amateur or student photography and are an inexpensive way to try out medium format photography.

A major problem with most folding cameras is deterioration of the bellows. After 50-100 years the bellows on these cameras have usually developed pinholes that will allow light into the camera and ruin the film. You can easily test a bellows by taking the camera into a dark room and shining a small flashlight into the bellows from the back. Move the flashlight around and flex the bellows since some light-leaks can be hidden by the folds. You can also look into the bellows from the back while moving a bright flashlight around the outside. If there are any holes you will see small dots of light coming through the bellows.

If there are only a few small holes and you want to take a roll of film to check the camera's operation, you can sometimes patch the bellows. This is done by smearing a little bit of light-tight filler into the hole. Black RTV silicon gasket sealer is a good choice for this. Put a small amount of the RTV on a small stick or blunt tooth pick and smear it over the hole. Leave the bellows extended until the RTV has cured. For larger holes, make a patch from a small piece of light-proof liner material and glue the patch over the hole. Tears in the outer fabric can be patched with suitably thin cloth tape.

Patching a bellows in this manner should always be considered a temporary fix. If the fabric in the bellows has started to develop holes the fabric is worn out and will continue to develop new light leaks over time. If the bellows is not light tight or the fabric is getting thin and starting to fall apart you should replace the bellows.

You can get a replacement from companies that make camera bellows. Do a search on the Internet or check the advertisements in Photography magazines for these companies. However, the cost of a newly made bellows is often more than the value of the camera and it is impractical in most cases to buy a bellows. As an alternative, you can sometimes find old inventory from a camera repair shop at very little cost. This is a good option if the bellows is still in good condition, will fit the camera, and is reasonably priced.

As an alternative to buying a bellows you can make your own. If you can measure accurately, draw straight perpendicular lines, and cut straight with scissors or a knife, you can make a replacement bellows. Like anything else, it takes practice to be able to fold the bellows so that the folds are straight and look nice. The bellows will work even if it doesn't look perfect, but the more practice you get, the closer you can get to a professional looking bellows. You will probably want to make several practice bellows first. Using plain cloth or a thin paper will allow you to make as many bellows as needed until you are confident that you can produce a bellows of the correct size and make the folds in the bellows properly.

Whether you have a new bellows made, find an old stock bellows, or make your own, you need to know how large of a bellows is needed. The information in this book will help you measure the bellows for the proper replacement.

The information in this book was determined empirically by studying numerous small bellows. It relies on most of the details for a proper bellows having already been determined by the camera manufacturer. Furthermore, there may be differences in terminology and approach to bellows design between this book and engineering textbooks. This approach has been used successfully to make new bellows and should work in most cases. Note, however, that there is not sufficient information to design a bellows for a camera you designed. If you are constructing your own camera this information may be useful, but be aware that there are other factors that may need to be considered for a home-built camera.

Overview

Parallel and Tapered Shapes

Camera bellows may be one of two basic types. If the front and rear openings of the bellows are the same size, the sections of the bellows will be parallel. If you cut a parallel bellows along a corner and lay it out flat, the cloth will be rectangular. If the front and rear openings in the bellows are different sizes the sections of the bellows will taper and have a trapezoid shape. When laid out flat, a tapered bellows will have a shape like that shown in Figure 1. Roll film and folding plate cameras will typically have a tapered bellows. This is the type of bellows described in this book.

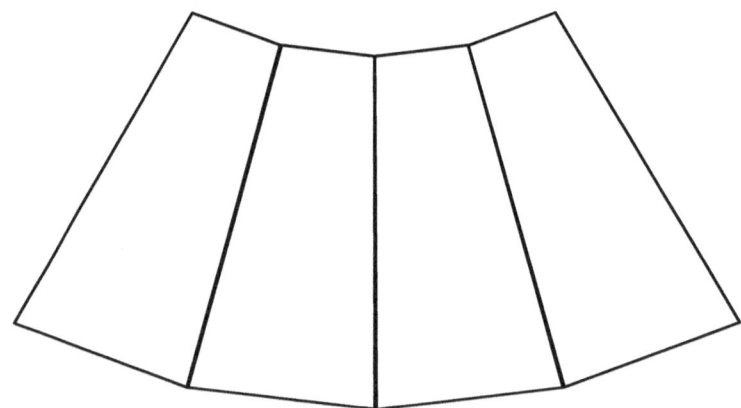

Figure 1 – Tapered bellows laid out flat

In order to avoid putting the seam at one of the corners, it is common for one of the sections to be split in half. This allows the seam to be located along the center of the bellows and hidden on the bottom. The shape of the cloth will be as shown in Figure 2.

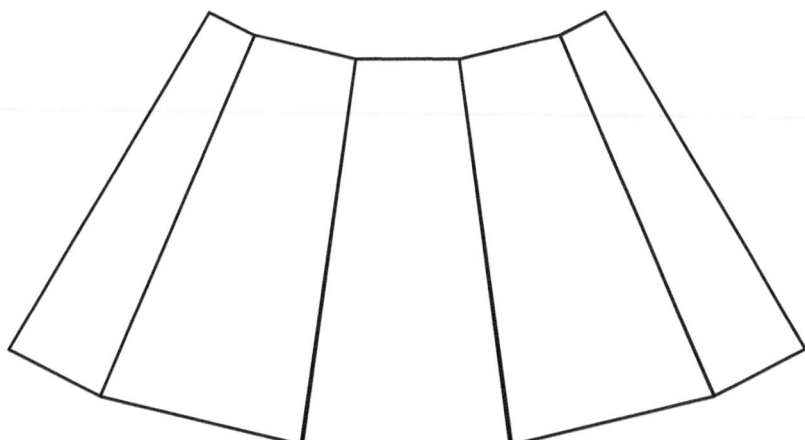

Figure 2 – Tapered bellows with one section halved

These patterns are for a bellows for a square film format such as 6x6 cm. If the camera is designed for a rectangular format, such as 6x9, the widths of the top and bottom are the same, but the widths of the two sides will be different. Although the corner edges are the same length, the angles of the trapezoid and the length along the center of each section will be different. This must be kept in mind when measuring a bellows for a rectangular film format.

Bellows Construction

A camera bellows usually has a sandwich construction. The inner layer is a liner of rubberized black cloth or similar material that is light-proof. The outer layer is a protective and decorative covering made of thin leather, cloth, vinyl or treated paper. The outer layer may also be light-proof but it isn't necessary for it to be so. As long as one of the layers is light-proof the bellows will function properly. On some bellows there is an additional layer of thin paper in between the cover and liner that may also be light-proof.

In between the liner and covering there is a series of thin stiffener ribs with a small space in between each rib. If you look closely at a bellows you can usually see the outline of the ribs in the outer layer. The ribs help give the bellows its shape and keep the fabric from sagging. The gaps between the ribs allow the cloth to easily fold around the ribs. The bellows cloth will fold wherever there is a gap in the ribs and remain straight where the ribs are located.

It is possible to make a bellows without ribs. If the material is flexible enough to fold yet stiff enough that it will hold a crease without sagging, then the material can simply be creased and folded into the proper shape. Some vinyl or paper materials impregnated or coated with light-proof material can be used this way. In most cases you will want to make the bellows using ribs as this will allow for a wider selection in materials.

To make a replacement bellows you need to carefully measure the length and width of the material, the number of folds, and the width of each fold. With this information you can then duplicate the original bellows. You cut out the liner and covering to match the bellows size, cut out and glue the ribs to the liner, lay the covering on, then fold the bellows into the proper form. Apart from removing the old bellows and installing the new one, that's really all there is to it.

If you were making your own camera, it would be necessary to know all about the various issues in designing a bellows. Fortunately, on an existing camera the designer has already developed the design for a proper bellows for the camera. Since you are replacing the bellows you can copy the original design without really knowing why it was done that way. However, in some situations, you will not be able to get exact measurements from the old bellows. The cloth will be difficult to lay flat due to the folds, and may be torn, frayed or stretched. Thus, it is useful to try and understand the bellows in detail. This will help you to understand what is important to copy exactly and what can be improvised. It also allows checking the measurements from the bellows and camera body to determine if they are consistent. If necessary, you could recalculate the bellows dimensions. The next few chapters contain a detailed description of the bellows so that you will understand how to get good measurements from an old bellows.

Bellows Dimensions

Figure 3 is a cross section view of a bellows showing the camera parts that affect the bellows dimensions. The important dimensions to understand are the length, width, and number and depth of each fold.

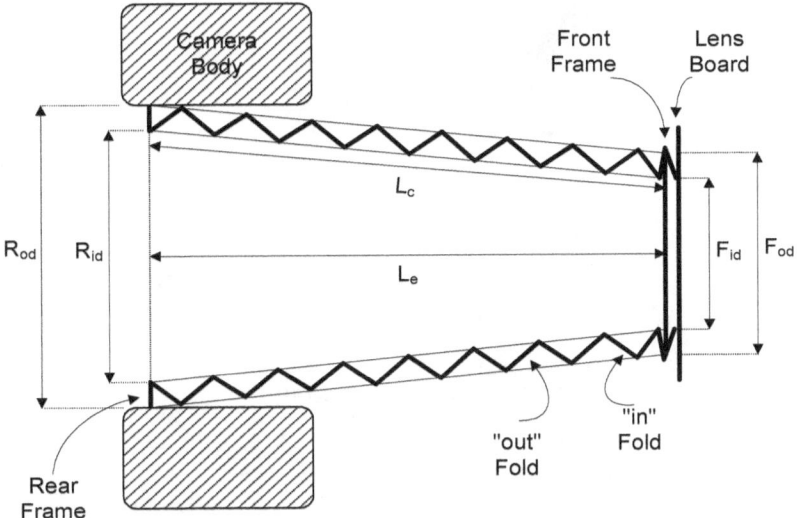

Figure 3 – Basic bellows dimensions

The dimensions given are as follows:

R_{od} Outside dimension of the rear frame of the bellows or camera body. This value may be different for adjacent sides.

R_{id} Inside dimension of the rear frame of the bellows or opening in the camera body. If the camera has a square film format, this value will be the same for all sides. For a rectangular film format, this value will be different for adjacent sides.

L_e Length of the bellows extension along the center of a bellows section.

L_c Length of the bellows along a corner between two sections. This will always be slightly longer than L_e on a tapered bellows.

F_{od} Outside dimensions of the front frame. This value may be different for adjacent sides.

F_{id} Inside dimension of the front frame. Usually this is the same as the opening in the frame for the lens/shutter.

Figure 4 shows the cross section when the bellows is collapsed.

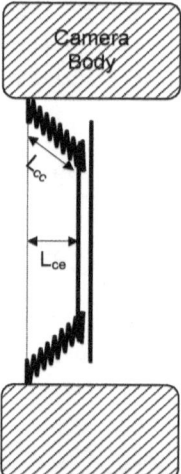

Figure 4 – Bellows folded up

L_{ce} Length of the bellows along the center when collapsed.

L_{cc} Length of the bellows along a corner between two sections when collapsed. This will always be slightly longer than L_{ce} on a tapered bellows.

Other dimensions can be easily calculated from these dimensions.

Variable Taper

If the difference between the inside and outside dimensions of the front frame is different than the difference on the rear frame, the taper of the bellows along the outside of the bellows will not be parallel with the taper on the inside. This means that at some point the width of the bellows folds must change. (See Figure 5) This situation is most commonly seen on longer bellows. On shorter bellows, the angle of the taper is usually sharp enough to clear the camera body without a change in the width of the folds.

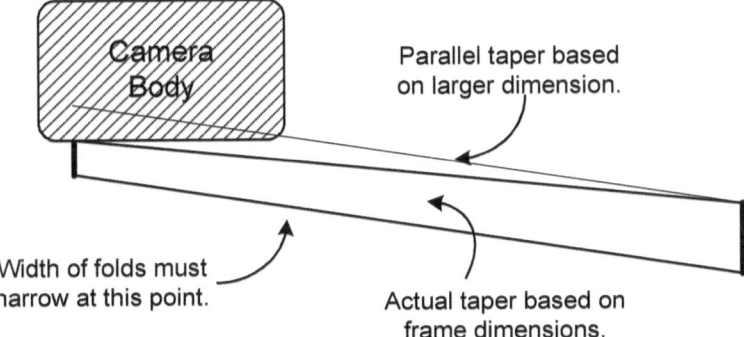

Figure 5 – Bellows with variable taper.

The bellows could have been constructed by shortening each fold by a small amount. However, the bellows designer most likely kept the folds the same up to the point where the taper would interfere with the camera body. At that point, the width of the folds is changed so that the bellows will fit inside the body. What you will see in that case is a set of narrower folds at the rear of the bellows. When measuring the folds of the bellows you should be aware of this possibility.

Bellows Length

The bellows extends from the rear frame at the film gate to the front frame located immediately behind the lens board (L_e). This is called the bellows extension. On a camera with self-erecting front, this distance will be approximately equal to the focal length of the lens minus the distance from the aperture diaphragm to the bellows front frame. On cameras that have a movable lens board, the extension must include the distance the lens board can move forward.

If you know the front and rear width and the bellows extension, you can calculate the center length of the adjacent sections and the length along the corners. Figure 6 shows the bellows in perspective. The two right triangles are formed from the line in the plane of the rear frame (*a*), the bellows extension along the center of the bellows (*b*), and the length along the center line of a section (*c*).

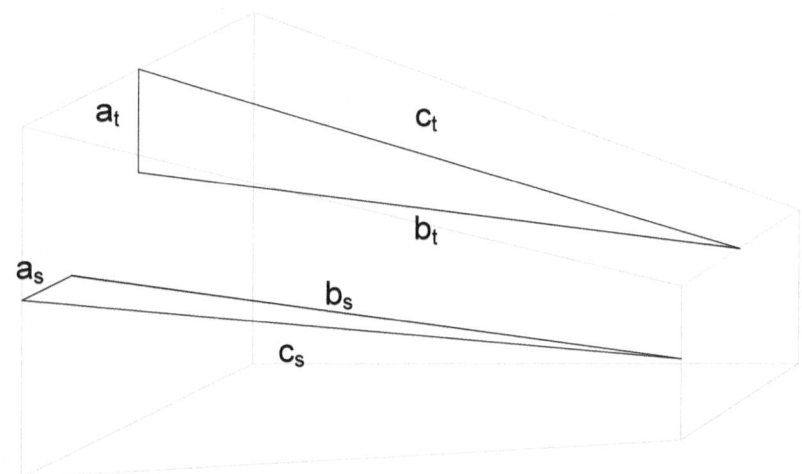

Figure 6 – Calculating taper from frame-to-frame distance

The length of *a* is calculated as one-half the difference between the widths of the front and rear. The length along a center of a bellows section is thus:

Two right triangles are also formed by the line in the plane of the rear frame (*a*), the length along the center line of a section (*c*), and the length along the corner as shown by Figure 7.

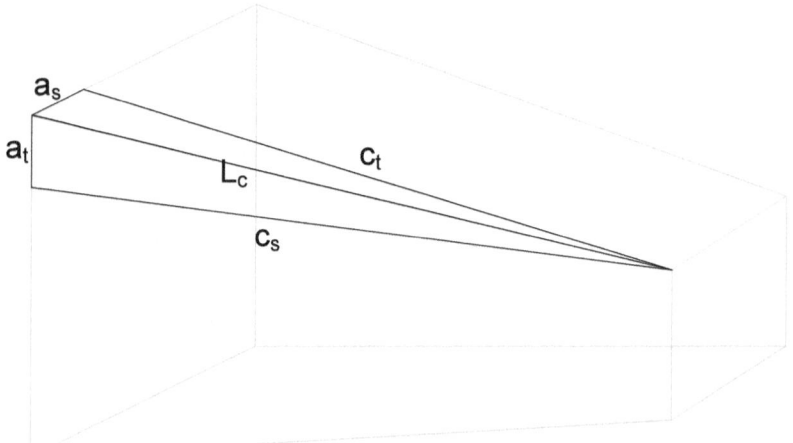

Figure 7 – Calculating bellows corner length.

The bellows length along the corners (L_c) can be calculated as:

This distance will be slightly longer than the length of the bellows along the center of a section due to the taper in the bellows. If the camera has a non-square film gate (e.g. 6x9 film format) the top and bottom of the bellows will be of a different length along the center line. However, the corner length will be the same for all sections regardless of the bellows shape.

Conversely, if you know the length along the corners, you can calculate the length along the center of each section. Thus you can use whichever measurements are easier to take from the camera and/or bellows.

Either the center length or the corner length can be used to construct a new bellows. However, if you base your measurements on the length along the corner, constructing a new bellows will be easier for non-square film formats.

The bellows needs to be long enough to stretch from the rear frame to the front frame without putting stress on the lens board or the places where the bellows is attached to the frame. To accomplish this, the overall length of the bellows material is made longer than the bellows extension. This allows the folds to remain partially folded even when the bellows is extended. A good approximation of the total length of the bellows material is 1.3 to 1.4 times the bellows extension. The actual value can be measured from the bellows if the bellows is intact and not stretched out of shape. Since the cloth may not lay flat and the edges may be frayed or uneven, most often you will need to calculate this value using a combination of other measurements. As described below, the best way to do this is to sum the widths of the folds and then add on as needed for the front and rear flaps.

Bellows Width

The width of the bellows at the front and rear is determined by the width of the respective frames and the way the bellows folds over the frames. The width of the bellows at the point where the bellows folds over the frame must obviously be the size of the frame (more or less). If the cloth folds over the frame a small amount must be added to account for the thickness of the cloth. Because the sections are tapered, the actual width of the bellows at the front and/or rear will be different than the width at the frame. The edge of the bellows will be narrower in front and wider at the rear than at the frames. The amount of difference will depend on the bellows taper. It is better to measure at the frames since the edges of the cloth may be frayed or cut away. As shown later, it is very easy to extend the length of the bellows to account for the material folded against the frames.

Typically, the inside dimension of the rear frame is the same as the film gate and is slightly smaller than the nominal film size. For example, a 6x6 format film will have a film gate of around 56mm width. The width of the bellows at the point where it attaches to the frame will be determined by the width of the film gate (R_{id}). The bellows material may fold over the frame, inside the body opening, or be attached in front of the frame. In any case, the width of the bellows at the rear edge is limited by the outside dimensions of the frame (R_{od}).

Similarly, the width of the bellows at the front is controlled by the width needed where the bellows attaches to the frame. If the material folds over the frame, the width of the bellows at the point where it contacts the frame must be equal or greater than the width of the front frame (F_{od}). The actual width at the front edge of the bellows will be slightly smaller than the outside dimension of the front frame.

Folds

The folds need to be shallow enough that they don't interfere with the image path. Given the length of the bellows extension and the maximum width of folds, the minimum number of folds the bellows needs can be determined by dividing the length by the maximum fold width. However the number of folds must be such that the bellows will fit into the space available inside the camera body when folded up. Thus while the minimum number of folds is determined by the maximum fold width, the maximum number of folds is determined by the thickness of the cloth and the space in the camera body.

The difference between the outside dimension of the rear frame (R_{od}) minus the inside dimension (R_{id}) determines how much space is available for the bellows folds at the rear of the bellows. The dimension may not be the same on the sides as on the top and bottom. The difference between the outside dimension of the front frame (F_{od}) and the inside dimension (F_{id}) determines the amount of space available for the folds at the front of the bellows. However, because the folds expand when the bellows is open, the depth of the folds when closed may be more than the maximum allowed by the frame.

16

Depending on the camera's design, the space available at the rear of the bellows may be less than the space available at the front. In many cases there will be attachments for the struts, body release for the shutter, and door latch that are inside the camera as well. The bellows folds cannot be allowed to interfere with those mechanisms. Thus, you often see a bellows where the width of the folds decreases towards the rear of the bellows. This results in a greater number of folds over a given distance at the rear of the bellows than at the front.

Folds will be described as "in" or "out" respective to the front of the bellows. If the fold is moving towards the center, it is an "in" fold. If moving away from the center, it is an "out" fold. "In" folds are usually shorter than "out" folds due to the taper of the bellows. This will be explained in more detail in a later section.

Number of folds and Thickness of Material

When folded the bellows must collapse into the available space within the camera body. The distance from the rear frame to the front frame (L_{cc}) determines the total amount of space for the folded bellows. As indicated before, the number of folds is determined by the combination of the bellows extension and the maximum depth of the folds. The thickness of the bellows material multiplied by the number of folds must be less than or equal to the space in the body.

Typically there will only be 10mm of space. If the bellows has twenty folds, the bellows material in that case can be no more than .5mm thick. If the material you use is thicker than the original bellows, you may encounter problems getting the bellows to fit into the camera.

Understanding Bellows Folds

Although at first bellows folds appear confusing and look difficult to make, it is actually easy to fold the bellows once you understand how the folds are made. In fact, it is more difficult to explain making the folds that it is to make them. To understand bellows folds it helps to make a half-bellows out of paper.

Triangular Folds

Take a rectangle of paper approximately 10x20cm (a half sheet of typing paper) and draw lines across the paper lengthwise every centimeter to produce 10 sections. Crease the paper in half lengthwise and fold it to make a right angle. Starting at the left edge, fold the paper underneath along the first line. Work from the edge towards the center but stop before reaching the center. Move to the right edge and fold the paper up along the first line. In other words, fold the paper one direction on the left half and the opposite direction on the right half. When one section is folded "out" the adjacent section is folded "in" at the same place. At the center, pinch the folds into a triangle shape so that the two half-folds overlap. Go to the left edge again and fold the paper in the opposite direction of the first fold and do the right section in the opposite direction as well. Repeat this along the length of the bellows until you reach the end of the paper. The result should look similar to that shown in the Figure 8.

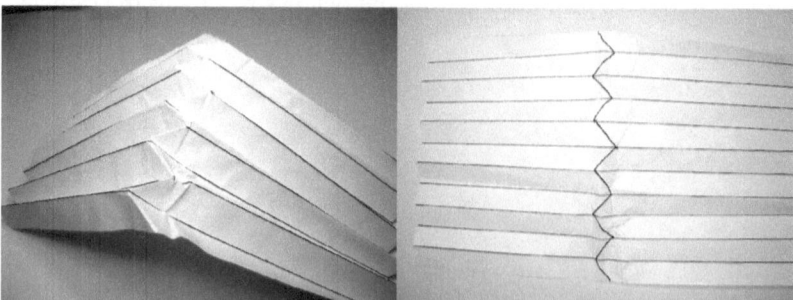

Figure 8 – Triangular bellows folds

If you open the paper flat and trace along the folds in the corners you will see a zig-zag line back and forth over the corner folds. On a parallel bellows, where all the folds are the same width, the angle of the corners is the same for each fold. On a tapered bellows, the angles on successive folds are not the same and as a result the widths of the folds are not the same. This is explained in more detail below.

Square Corners

Triangular corners like the ones you just made are created when the folds in a section are in the opposite direction of the folds in the adjacent section. If the folds on adjacent sections are identical in direction the result is a square corner fold. You can see the difference by making another half-bellows out of paper. Draw the lines on the paper as before. This time, fold all the way across the paper in the same direction as if you were making a paper fan. To make the corners, you push the paper down into the corner as shown in Figure 9. This type of bellows fold is common on cameras from the 19th century but does not appear to have ever been used on smaller folding cameras.

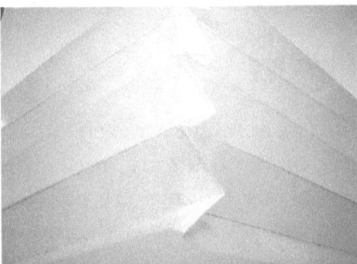

Figure 9 – Square bellows corners.

Fold Ribs and Gaps

In a sandwich type construction, each fold has a separate piece of rib material with a small gap between the folds. Even the thinnest material cannot fold over without some space lengthwise. As shown in Figure 10 the point where the fold occurs will be slightly rounded even if it looks straight. To allow the folds to flex, a gap is left in between each pair of ribs. While the ribs are relatively stiff, the liner and covering material can be more flexible and make a sharper fold. When calculating the length of the bellows from the folds, the actual width of each fold is the width of the rib plus the gap.

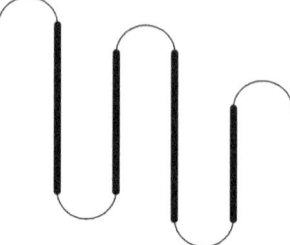

Figure 10 – Gaps between stiffeners.

The amount of gap between ribs is usually at least twice the thickness of the material, although sometimes it is less. Typically, you will see a gap of three times the thickness. For example, if the material is .5mm thick, the gaps will probably be 1.5mm wide. If you cannot precisely measure the gaps, a value of 1.5 to 2 mm will give a good approximation.

Alternating Widths on a Tapered Bellows

Because the sections of tapered bellows are at an angle to each other, the widths of the folds vary and the angles of the folds are not equal. Figure 11 shows the folds when the sides of the bellows are parallel. The widths of the angles and folds are the same for out folds and in folds.

Note: The angles and dimensions in these drawings are for illustration and are approximate. The angle of the corners when viewed from the front of a folded bellows is 45°. However, when the bellows is laid out flat, you will see an angle of approximately 50°. Since the corner fold moves laterally along the bellows, the actual angle between the corners and the sides is stretched slightly as the bellows is stretched out.

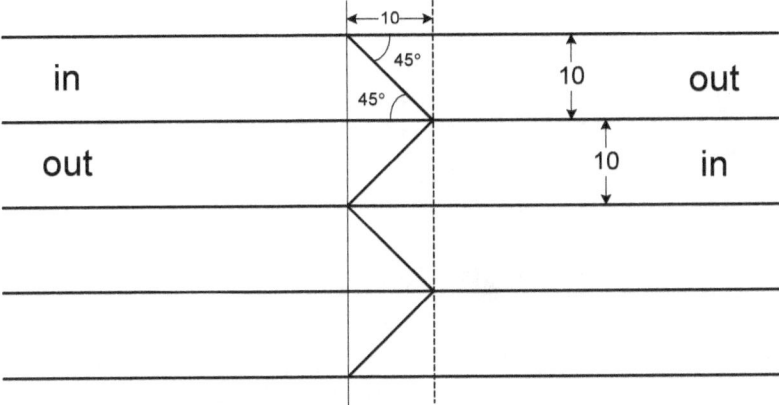

Figure 11 – Corner angles in a square bellows.

Figure 12 shows the folds and angles when the bellows is tapered. The sides are not straight but sit at a slight angle to each other. As a result the angles of the folds to the corners are different and the widths of the folds alternate between wide and narrow.

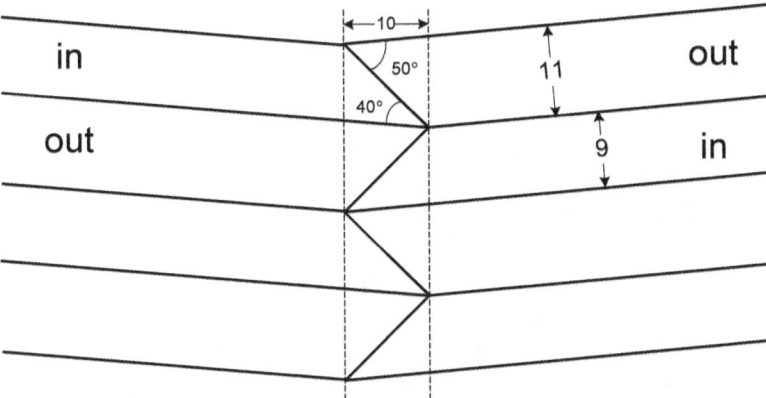

Figure 12 – Corner angles in a tapered bellows.

Another factor that affects the widths of the folds is the width along the corners. (See Figure 13) If the bellows taper is different at the front and rear of the bellows, the folds must change in width at some point along the bellows. This requires that either the distance along the corner between the sides, or the angle of the corners, changes.

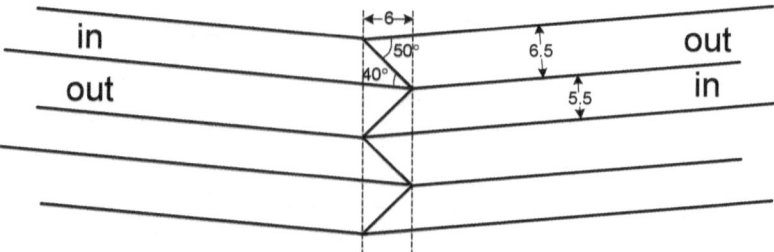

Figure 13 – Corner angles affected by corner width.

Although possible, it would be complicated to precisely calculate the angles and widths from the bellows taper. Fortunately, when you are copying an existing bellows you merely need to measure the exact width of the folds and duplicate those widths. As you fold the bellows, the corners will take on the correct shape automatically. The flexibility of the bellows material and the gaps around the folds allow the angles to shift slightly as needed.

For any segment of the bellows where all fold pairs are the same length, you can also estimate the difference between the folds as T / N where T is the taper of the bellows and N is the number of folds. This is the amount that the bellows must step out/in for each fold. Calculate the total amount of taper by taking one-half the difference between the inside dimension of the rear and front frames: $T = (R_{id} - F_{id})/2$. To determine the relative widths of the in and out folds take the width of a pair, subtract the step size and divide by two to get the width of the smaller fold. For example, if there are 16 folds, and T is 24 mm, then the step is 1.5 mm. If the width of a pair of folds is 13.5 mm, this would give folds of 7.5 mm and 6 mm. If the gap between ribs is 1.5 mm, then the width of the ribs should be about 6 and 4.5 mm.

Because of the alternating widths of the folds, it is easiest to measure the folds in pairs rather than individually. Typically the same ratio between the folds will repeat the length of the bellows. Once you determine the width of a pair of folds, you can simply multiply this by one-half the number of folds to determine the length of material spanned by the folds. This value then becomes the basis for calculating the actual length of the bellows material.

There may be an exception to the alternating widths at some point on the bellows. Most commonly this occurs at the rear of the bellows where the bellows taper is reduced to fit inside the camera body. In addition, the amount of the step for each fold will be different between the adjacent sections on a bellows for a rectangular film format. Thus you must measure folds for the top and side individually.

Stiffener Rib Shape

Stiffener ribs can either project into the corners or be cut off at the corners (see Figure 14). When the ribs project into the corners they will have a sharp point. When cut off, the ribs will have a trapezoid shape that follows the taper of the corners. When making a bellows by hand, it is easier to make all the ribs without the pointed sections that project into the folds even if the original bellows has the points. On a larger bellows the projections into the folds will help the corners keep their shape. However, on a small bellows for a roll film camera this is not needed. The corners will retain a good shape even without the stiffness of the rib material. If you want to make pointed ribs, draw the points between the leading edge of a rib in one section with the rear edge of the associated rib on the adjacent section. These lines will approximate the path of the corner folds. Leave a small gap between the points and the ribs on the adjacent section so that the sharp points of the ribs do not poke into the bellows cloth.

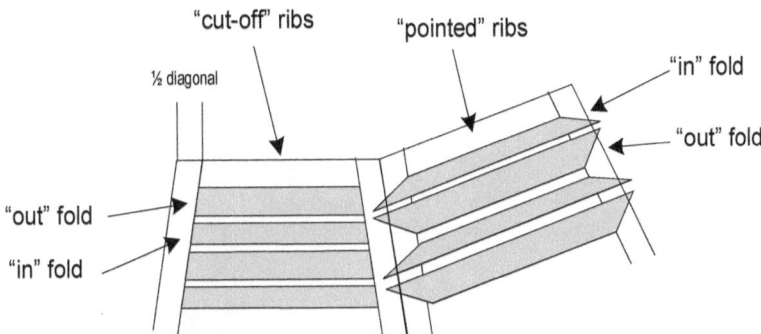

Figure 14 – Stiffener types

The point where the ribs are cut off is determined by the width of the diagonals of the folds. The easiest way to calculate the appropriate amount is from the diagonals along the front frame. This is shown in a later section.

Practice Tapered Bellows

If you want to practice making the folds you can make a whole bellows out of paper. Draw a trapezoid onto thin paper and cut along the left, top and bottom sides. Fold the paper over along the right edge and trace the top, bottom and edge. Cut the top and bottom sides that you just made. Fold the paper back out flat and then fold the double-trapezoid over again on the right edge. Trace the top, bottom and edge and then cut along the top, bottom and right sides. Crease the paper across each section every 5-6mm stopping the creases about 3mm from the corners. Fold the four sections into a tapered box and use a strip of tape to hold the corners together. You can then practice making the folds in the bellows. You will find it is best to start each fold by pinching the paper together in the center of the section and then working your way towards the corners. Pinch the corners into a triangle then move to the next fold.

Frame Attachment

The shape of the frames and whether the material goes over or inside the frames affects the layout of the bellows ribs. Some frames are rectangular while others are octagonal. There are also two ways the material can attach to the frame. The material can attach at the same distance from the front edge on all sections, or it can attach at a different distance on adjacent sections.

Octagonal Front Frame

Figure 15 shows how the bellows typically attaches to an octagonal front frame. The dotted line shows the location of the frame in relation to the bellows cloth. The shaded areas are the ribs. The small line drawings at the top and side show how the cloth folds over the frame. The diagonals of the front frame match the triangular corners and the width of the ribs where they meet the frame is approximately the same as the longer sides of the frame. On many bellows the extra "in" folds on two sides (or top and bottom) are cut away and is shown by the hatched portion of the figure.

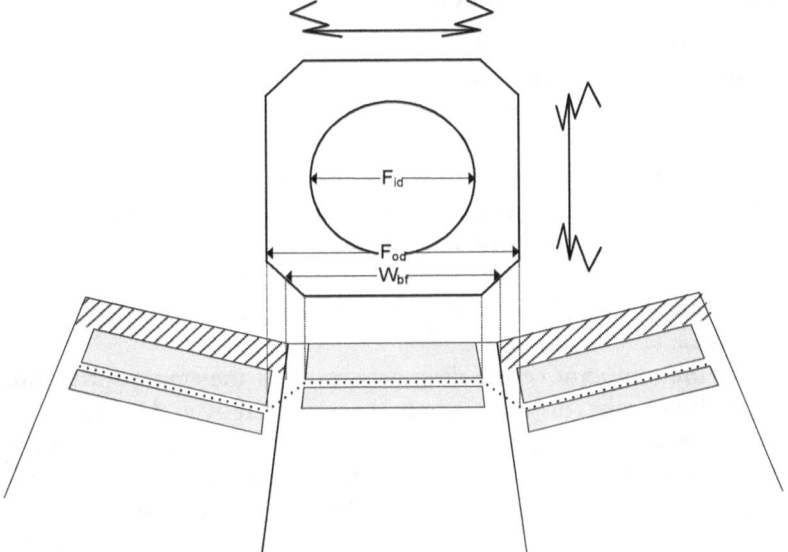

Figure 15 – Front attachment for octagonal frame.

The top of the bellows (center section in the figure) attaches to the frame at a different distance from the front edge of the cloth than the sides. Because folds on adjacent sections go in opposite directions, only one of the sections can fold over the frame at any given fold. The point of the "out" fold on the bellows top where it folds over the frame would normally match an "in" fold on the adjacent sections. In order to have all sections of the bellows fold over the frame, the two sections must be shifted forward by one fold.

In addition, because the first fold on the sides is usually cut away, it may appear that the sides of the bellows are a different length than the top and bottom. When drawing out the pattern, however, make all the sections the same length along the corners and then cut away any excess material after attaching the bellows to the frame.

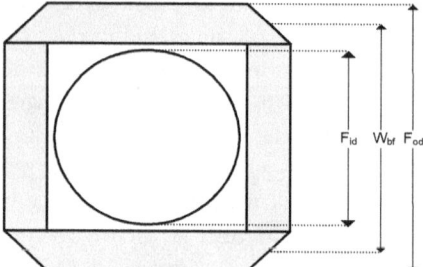

Figure 16 – Frame folds for octagonal frame.

Figure 16 shows the view from the front. Note how the corners match the diagonals of the frame. The value of W_{bf} is the width of the cloth from corner to corner at the point where the cloth wraps over the frame. This value is equal to the width of the long side plus the diagonal of the corner fold. However, because of the bellows taper, both the top and side cannot have an identical distance at this point. On a rectangular film format, you can determine each distance individually. On a square film format, you can simply take the longer of the two values and apply it to both the top and sides. The difference in length will be very small.

Since the midpoint of the diagonals matches the actual corner line of the bellows, the distance along the diagonal will determine the amount of space on each side of the corner where the ribs are cut off. Because the diagonal is moving along the length of the bellows, the amount of setback of the ribs from the corners will be slightly less than one-half the length of the diagonal. The actual value should be approximately equal to the hypotenuse of a right triangle formed by one-half the diagonal and the corner line as shown in Figure 17. Often this value will be the difference between the inside and outside dimensions of the front frame. For an octagonal front frame, this can be measured directly from the frame. Check the value by measuring the distance of the diagonal and space on the bellows cloth. They should be the same.

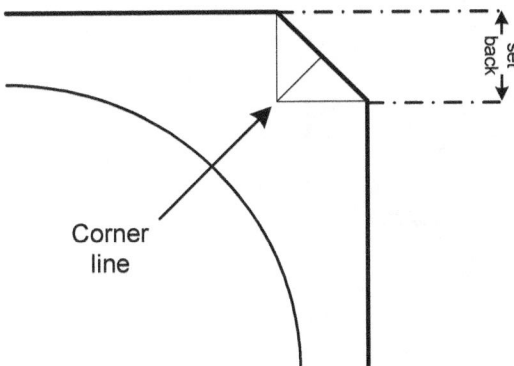

Figure 17 – Bellows corners

Rectangular Front Frame

Figure 18 shows the front of the bellows for a typical rectangular frame. In this type of arrangement, the front edge of the bellows is even all the way around and the cloth meets the frame at the same point on both top and side. The first "out" fold on the sides is folded away from the frame instead of overlapping the frame. The front flap is used instead as the means of attaching the cloth to the frame. This type of bellows is commonly found on older Kodak cameras.

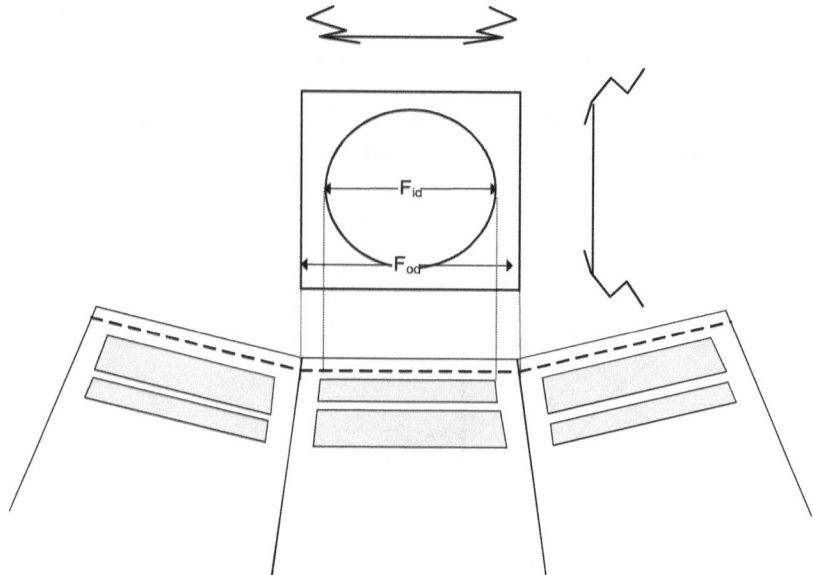

Figure 18 – Frame attachment for rectangular frame.

Figure 19 shows how this looks from the front. For this type of bellows, you can simply measure the width of the front frame on top and side and then set the bellows width at the point of the front frame to that value.

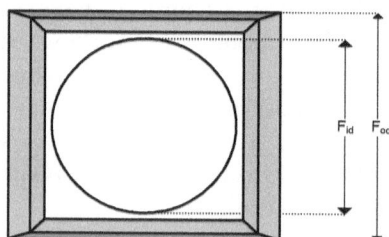

Figure 19 – Front folds for rectangular frame.

Because there is no diagonal section of the front frame, you must measure the amount the ribs are set back from the cloth. A typical value is in the range of 3 to 5 mm. If you can't get an exact measurement, use 3 mm. The width of the rib at the front frame is then equal to the width of the frame minus twice the value of the set back. As shown in Figure 18, you can probably use the inside dimension of the frame as the width of the rib and then calculate the set back amount as one-half the difference between the outside and inside dimensions of the frame.

Rear Attachment Through the Camera Body

The rear attachment of the bellows is often made by passing the bellows through the body opening and folding the cloth outwards. The width of the bellows, not counting the corners, will be the same as the width of the opening in the camera body. Usually this is the same or very close to the size of the film gate. The corners are folded up into a dimple or cut-out in the corners of the frame.

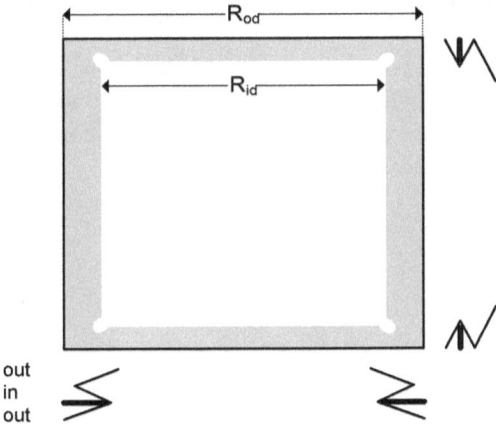

Figure 20 – Rear attachment through the body.

The amount of material past the body opening depends on the available space in the body around the opening and where the fold is placed. Often the camera will have more space on the sides than on the top and bottom. This is convenient since on one section the last fold will correspond to an "out" fold while the last fold on the adjacent section will correspond to an "in" fold. The difference in distance will allow the width of the corresponding fold to match the width of the frame and thus will not project into the image path. The point of attachment, however, will be shifted slightly forward from an adjacent section so that the flaps both fold outward.

Another type of attachment is possible by making three folds on the side spanning the same length as four folds on the top. The different number of folds causes the edges of the bellows to be even across the rear.

When the bellows passes through the frame this way, the measurement of the width should be made at the point the bellows is in contact with the frame. Like on the octagonal front, the edges may be of differing distance from the point of attachment.

Rear Attachment In Front of Camera Body

The rear attachment of the bellows may also be made in front of the body opening. Sometimes the bellows is attached to a frame that is clamped to the body (as on Kodak folders) or the bellows may simply be glued to the body.

For this type of attachment you can measure the edge of the bellows if it is not frayed or destroyed in removing the bellows from the camera. The width of the bellows at the edge should be the same as the outside dimension of the rear frame.

Seams

When the bellows material is folded into a tube there will be a seam where the edges of the cloth overlap. There will be two seams, one for the liner and one for the covering. The seams must be arranged so that the extra thickness at the seam does not make the bellows difficult or impossible to fold into the camera.

On older cameras you will usually see the liner and covering seams go down the middle of the material on opposite sides of the bellows. The liner seam is on top and hidden by the cover. The cover seam is on the bottom and hidden by the drop-down bed. This is shown in Figure 21.

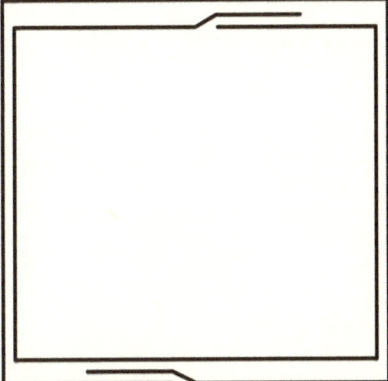

Figure 21 - Center seams on top and bottom

An alternative arrangement is to put both seams on the bottom. This will only work if the material is very thin. When both seams are on the bottom they should be slightly offset from each other as shown in Figure 22.

Figure 22 - Center seams on bottom.

It is also possible to put the seams at the corners. In this arrangement the seams should be at opposite corners as shown in Figure 23.

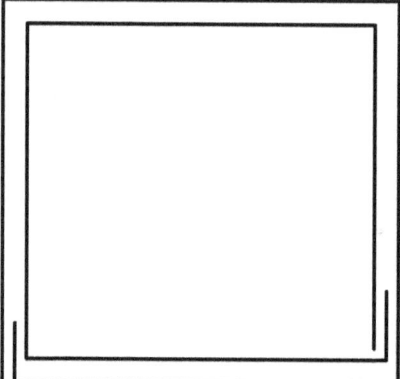

Figure 23 - Corner seams on opposite corners

When using a center seam the bellows pattern must be drawn with one section cut in half and the seam area added to one of the half sections. When a corner seam is used the seam tab is simply added to one side of the overall pattern.

Tools

You will need some basic camera repair tools to remove the bellows from the camera. Most of the tools are things you already have or are readily available at a hardware or department store.

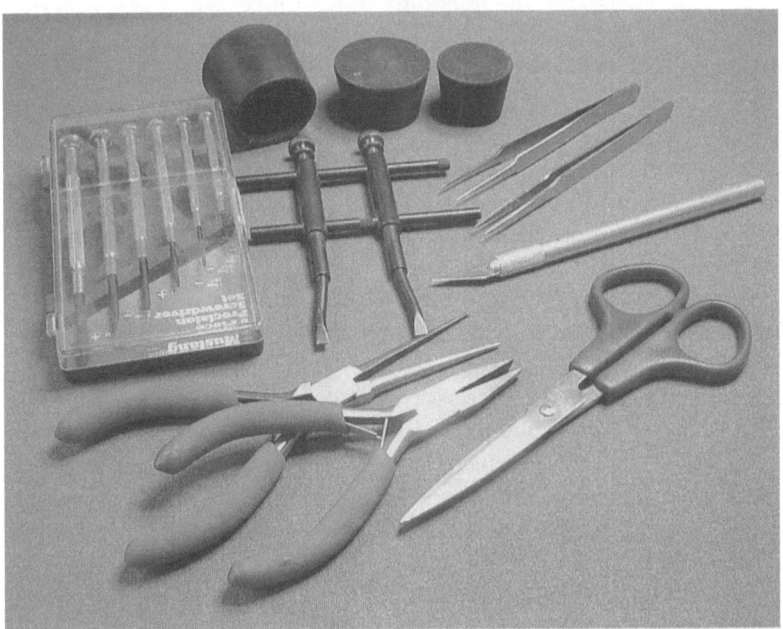

Basic Camera Tools

A set of small screwdrivers is needed. The inexpensive type in a plastic blue box will work. However, if you are going to be working on several cameras, it is worth the expense to purchase a good set of jeweler's screwdrivers. Many camera screws are non-standard. If needed, grind or file down tips to make a precise fit. Tweezers are also needed to handle the small parts you may encounter. Needle nose pliers are also very useful for pulling apart stubborn parts, but not necessary for most cameras.

You will need some type of lens spanner wrench. The typical adjustable lens spanner wrench has two vertical pieces with screwdriver like tips that slide along a bar. These may be difficult to locate since hardware stores don't carry them. Photography stores may have them available, however. As an alternate, you can use snap ring pliers or small needle nose pliers. You can also make a lens spanner by cutting away the end of a rigid paint scraper leaving two small tips to fit into the retaining ring slots.

A small rubber furniture leg cup or rubber stopper is also useful for removing and installing the retaining ring. Once you have the ring loosened, use the cup on the ring. This helps avoid accidentally poking a hole in the bellows or scratching the lens should the spanner wrench slip. If the rear lens element extends past the retaining ring, use a rubber cup to avoid pressing down on the lens. If the lens is recessed, you can use a rubber stopper instead. Because you have to reach into the bellows, it's useful to make a tool with a piece of rubber stuck on the end of a wooden dowel instead of a stopper.

Knife and/or scissors and cutting mat

To cut materials you can use scissors, hobby knife, or utility knife. The simple box cutter type tool with a replaceable single-edge razor is a very good choice. It is helpful to have both scissors and a knife since some materials have long edges and are best cut with a knife while other materials, such as fabric, are better cut with scissors. A rolling wheel type cutter can also be used, but a simple knife will usually be better. A good flat cutting surface such as a self-healing mat is helpful, but a piece of poster board will work as well.

Ruler and Square

A ruler with gradations to .5mm is needed to make precise measurements of the bellows and frames. A set of calipers are also useful, but not necessary. Most bellows dimensions can be rounded to .5mm without any problem.

You can draw the patterns on a computer or by hand. If drawing by hand, a set square or T-square is needed to make perpendicular and parallel lines. One of the small drafting sets containing right triangles, ruler and protractor would be sufficient. A draftsman's compass is also useful.

Clamps

Small spring clamps are useful for holding parts of the bellows together while the adhesive dries. The large binder clips sold at office supply stores work well as do the spring clips available at hardware stores.

Solvents and Lubricants

It will usually be necessary to dissolve the old glue on the camera body or frame. Alcohol or lacquer thinner works fine for this. To clean old grease or oil from moving body parts you can use naphtha. If you need to lubricate struts, shutter release button or hinges, use a thin oil such as watch oil or gun trigger oil. Use oil sparingly and wipe away any excess. Usually the struts on self-erecting cameras will not need lubrication to work properly. However, if there is rust on some parts, a tiny amount of oil will usually help. Do NOT put oil on the shutter unless you know shutter repair. If the shutter is not running properly it most likely needs cleaning.

Bellows Materials

A major challenge for the amateur bellows maker is finding the right materials in small quantities and low cost. You need very thin material that is stiff enough to hold a crease and strong enough to be folded and unfolded many times. A small bellows may have anywhere from ten to twenty folds and the thickness of the cloth gets multiplied by the number of folds. Thus, you need to make sure the material you use is thin enough to fit in the camera.

Total thickness

To find out how much space you have for the bellows, leave the camera folded up, open the back and measure the distance between the front frame and film gate. Although the bellows can collapse slightly into the inside and take a little bit more room than the measurement, if at all possible you want the entire bellows to sit flat inside the camera. Typically, the combined thickness of the bellows materials, stiffeners strips and adhesive can only be about .5mm (.020") in order for the bellows to easily fold up into the camera. In other words, you need a very thin material for both liner and covering.

To check your materials to see if they are thin enough, take a piece of the liner, covering and stiffener material and fold it as many times as needed for the bellows. Press the stack of material down as much as you can and then measure the total height. The total should be less than or equal to the distance you measured inside the camera with the original bellows folded up.

Liner Cloth

The original bellows probably used a very thin (.008 inch) black rubberized cloth for the liner. This is the most appropriate material for hand-made bellows but it may be difficult to locate this material from retailers at a low cost. Usually, you only need a small piece and the cost will be appropriate and still considerably less than a manufactured replacement bellows. However, you will probably need to make several bellows before you gain sufficient skill to make a correct bellows with a nice appearance. At the normal retail cost it can be very expensive to practice making bellows. You can practice using plain broadcloth or paper. Once you know you can make the bellows correctly, you can switch to using the more expensive type of material. If you cannot locate thin rubberized cloth at a low cost there are some inexpensive alternatives.

One alternative source of material is a film changing bag. If you buy a new changing bag, the cost of material may be about the same as ordering the specialty material. However, if you have an old bag that you aren't using anymore, or can find a used bag at a flea market, you can get bellows material for very little cost this way. A changing bag is also a good choice if you cannot locate a retailer who can sell you the cloth in small quantities.

Another alternative material you may be able to use is called black-out curtain. This material is used to make liners for curtains where the room needs to be darkened. You can find this material anywhere curtain material is sold or you can buy it by the yard at most fabric stores. You may also find this in larger camera stores. There are two potential problems with black-out curtain that you need to be aware of. The first problem is the color. Although this material is manufactured in various colors, you may not be able to find the material in black. If you can locate white colored material, you can paint it black using inexpensive acrylic craft paint. Thin the paint one-to-one with water, apply two coats on the cloth side of the curtain liner. It is not necessary to paint the treated side since it will go to the inside of the bellows. Once you cut the cloth it will have a white edge. Use a black felt-tip marker to blacken the edge.

The second potential problem with black-out curtain is the thickness of the material. Some black-out curtain material is .016" thick, or about twice as thick as regular bellows cloth. Remember that the total thickness of the combined materials can only be about .020" and thus with this cloth you need to use very thin covering material or it will be too thick. When combined with a 4 mil vinyl or thin broadcloth, black-out curtain will work for many cameras. Be sure to test the total thickness of your materials before constructing the bellows.

One other readily available alternative is the type of plastic bag used to hold photographic sheet film or paper. If you do your own enlarging you may already have some of these bags available. The bags are also available for purchase at most photography stores. A 5x7 size bag will make two bellows for 6x6 or smaller format. A bag for 8x10 will make two 6x9 or three 6x6 bellows. Although this material is light-proof, it usually has a glossy surface and cannot be used for the interior of the bellows. If you don't mind having a shiny black plastic bellows, you can use this material for the outer covering with flat black broadcloth on the interior. Alternatively, you can laminate this material onto a very thin piece of broadcloth or vinyl to make a piece of light-proof material that is around .008" thick. It is usually best to laminate the plastic to the outer covering rather than the liner.

To laminate the bag, cut the bag along the seams and lay it out flat. Tape the corners down so that the material does not curl up. Use some spray-on adhesive to make a solid coating of adhesive on the plastic and then press a piece of cloth, vinyl or paper down onto it. Make sure to smooth out any wrinkles in the material. Roll over the material with a piece of pipe or a rolling pin to press the materials together. Let the adhesive dry and then you can cut out the bellows shape from the material.

Covering

For the outer covering, any suitably thin material that will hold a crease and fold and unfold repeatedly will work. You can use lightweight broadcloth or rip-stop nylon. These materials are inexpensive, very thin, and allow you to make a nice looking bellows in any color you want. A faux suede material is another fabric that can be used. Just make sure it is thin enough to fold up inside the camera.

Thin leather or other animal skins from a leather supplier is another choice. These types of material may vary in thickness, so be sure to check across the entire piece of material.

Another good material that is readily available and inexpensive is self-adhesive vinyl surface or shelf covering. This is a thin, durable, self-adhesive vinyl that is sold in most hardware, home-improvement, and craft stores. Most of the material that you see sold in stores has some type of printed pattern. Typically what you see is material with floral patterns, stripes, faux metal and marble finishes. For those with rather eccentric tastes, those might make some interesting looking bellows. However, you can also find solid colors with a matte finish and light pebble grain texture as well as imitation leather look. You may need the retailer to order this for you since it is often not carried in stock.

Vinyl or leatherette from a notebook, photo album or photo storage box is another possible type of covering material. Many of these have an imitation leather pattern that is similar to the original bellows. The paper sold as book covers is another choice. Often this material is a laminate of paper and vinyl and is very strong even though made out of paper.

Stiffener Ribs

Most books on bellows making for large cameras recommend using 67lb cover stock or similar material for the ribs. If the covering and liner are thin enough, this is a good choice. This type of material may be too thick for a small camera bellows. Since the ribs are glued onto the liner the glue will add some stiffness to the material. Thus you don't need to have a very heavy or stiff material to work for a small bellows.

A good material for small bellows ribs is Kraft paper. This is a 60lb paper but is about half the thickness of cover stock. This type of material is used to make yellow or brown clasp envelopes that you probably have received in the mail. You can cut the ribs from the envelope. You can also purchase this material in rolls anywhere packaging or art supplies are sold. If you plan on using a computer to draw the patterns, you can cut the Kraft paper into a letter size piece and it should fit through the printer.

Adhesives

Any type of water-based household glue can be used to glue the ribs onto the bellows cloth. Glue sticks or glue pens are an inexpensive and convenient choice. Simply swipe the back of the stiffener rib with the glue stick and press in place. Glue from a bottle should be brushed on to make a thin even layer. Remember that water-based glue will take longer to cure. Let the glue dry completely before attempting to fold the bellows.

For the seams of the bellows, and to attach the bellows to the frames, use contact cement. To attach the covering either brush on contact cement or use one of the spray-on adhesives such as those sold for mounting photographs.

If you are using a self-adhesive vinyl covering, you can lay the covering in place and then press down to make a permanent bond. However, it is a good idea to add some glue or contact cement to the seams. The light-tack adhesive on the vinyl is often not enough to hold the seams and edges together.

Whatever adhesive you choose it is a good idea to first test it on scrap pieces of the bellows materials. Make sure the adhesive will hold and also that it does not damage the material. Water based glue may not hold on plastic or vinyl. Contact cement or spray-on adhesive may have solvents that can damage vinyl or rubber.

Steps in Making a Bellows

The steps to make a replacement bellows are as follows:

1. Remove the old bellows from the camera.
2. Determine dimensions of the bellows.
3. Make patterns for the liner, cover and ribs.
4. Make the form
5. Cut out the material.
6. Fold the liner around the form.
7. Cut out the ribs and glue them to the lining.
8. Glue the covering to the liner.
9. Make the folds in the bellows.
10. Install the new bellows in the camera.
11. Test the bellows for light leaks.

This method is the classic way of making a replacement bellows and was taught to professional repairmen in the past. Thus, it's a way of making a bellows that is known to work. Each of the steps is described in detail in the following sections.

There are some variations from this method. First, you may not need to make a form. It is possible to lay out the cloth flat, glue on the ribs, glue on the covering and then fold the bellows into a tube. This puts the seams for both the covering and liner on the same section of the bellows. If you choose this method, be sure the seams are side by side and not directly on top of each other. Second, if the materials you are using are stiff enough, you can avoid cutting and gluing ribs. Instead, simply crease the material with a scribing wheel or embossing tool and then make the folds.

Removing the Old Bellows

Camera manufactures used a variety of techniques to attach the bellows to the camera. You will have to study the camera to discover how the bellows is attached and the best way to remove the old bellows.

You will need to first remove the shutter and lens from the camera. The lens is mounted into the shutter and both will come out together without having to be separated. However, you may want to unscrew the rear lens first in order to reduce the possibility of scratching the lens when removing the shutter retaining ring. The most typical arrangement is that the shutter is held to the lens board by a single retaining ring at the rear. There will be two or four slots in the ring. You may see multiple rings from the back. The outermost ring is the one that holds the shutter in place. (See Figure 24) Open the camera back and unscrew the retaining ring with a lens spanner wrench. If you don't have a lens spanner, you can use small needle-nose pliers, snap-ring pliers, or a pair of scissors as a substitute. With the retaining ring loose, carefully open the front and reach in and pull the shutter out. On self-erecting type cameras, be careful to not let the front pop open since the shutter can be thrown out.

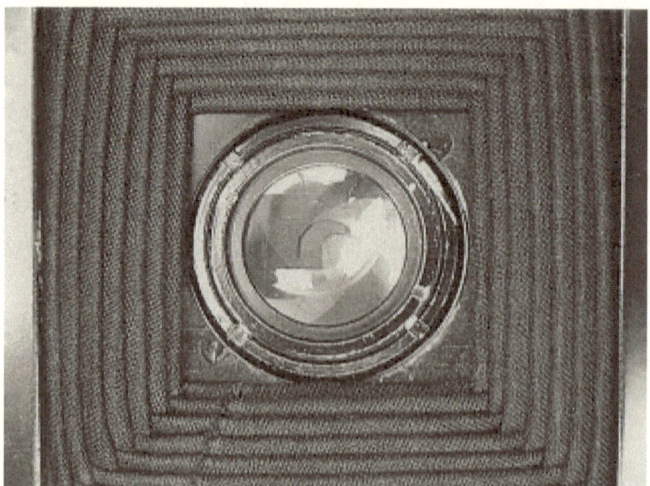

Figure 24 –Lens is held with a retaining ring from the rear.

The bellows is attached to a front frame that is clamped to the lens board. Sometimes the front frame is held in place by the shutter retaining ring. In that case, once you remove the shutter the front frame will become separated from the lens board. On other cameras, especially Kodak cameras, the front frame is held on with small rivets. These rivets have to be punched out once the shutter is removed from the lens board. Cut the bellows free from the frame, preserving as much of the old bellows as possible. Try to slip a thin knife or razor blade between the bellows and frame and cut the old glue loose. This will help to preserve the front edge of the bellows. A small amount of alcohol placed on the bellows where it attaches to the frame will usually soften the glue and make it easier to remove the bellows from the frame.

The rear of the bellows may be attached to a removable frame or may be glued directly onto the camera body. Feel along the inside edge of the film gate and see if there are small tabs that fold over. Pull these tabs out straight and the frame will lift away from the camera body. Carefully cut the bellows away from the frame. Clean the old glue from the frame before attaching the new bellows.

On other cameras, the bellows is clamped to the body with a removable film gate. Look inside the film chambers for small screws that hold the frame in place. Remove the screws and pry out the film gate being careful not to bend it. Cut the bellows free from the camera body, preserving as much of the old bellows as possible. Clean off any old glue from the body and film gate.

If there are no screws, look for tabs that fold over and hold the film gate to the camera. You can pull the tabs up and remove the frame, but this sometimes this is very difficult and may damage the camera body. There are also some cameras where the rear bellows frame or film gate is assembled with rivets. It may not be possible to remove the film gate without major disassembly of the camera. In either case, the best thing to do is carefully cut around the edge of the bellows without removing the frame. You can install the new bellows by attaching the bellows to the front of the camera body around the film gate using contact cement.

With the bellows out of the camera, check for any signs of rust on the frame or body. Clean off the old glue and rust, and use touch-up paint where necessary. Glue can usually be softened with either alcohol or lacquer thinner. Rust may need to be removed with a small wire brush. Be careful when using solvents not to allow the solvents to run onto parts of the camera that could be damaged.

This is also a good time to clean the inside of the camera and clean and lubricate any sticky struts, shutter release, or other levers that are normally difficult to reach.

Measuring Bellows Dimensions

In order to draw patterns for the bellows and ribs, the following dimensions need to be determined.

1. Overall length of material from front to rear edges
2. Width at the front edge.
3. Width at the rear edge.
4. Number of folds
5. Width of each fold
6. Gap between each fold.

Bellows Length

You can begin by measuring the length of the bellows along the corners or the center of a section. Remember that for a rectangular film format, the center measurement will be different on adjacent sections. The difference, however, is usually in the range of 1-2mm. As explained earlier, if you have one of the two lengths you can calculate the other.

A different strategy is to find the length between the frame attachment points and then extend the length the amount needed for the material outside the frames. This overcomes the problem of the front and rear edges being different or torn.

If you measure the width of each fold you can sum the measurements together to get the length spanned by the folds. This is the best way to determine the length. You need to measure the folds anyway, and once you have that measurement, calculating the overall length is simple. This is the recommended way of determining the length.

Bellows Width

As with the length, you can attempt to measure the bellows width from the edge of the cloth, but will most likely encounter a problem. It will probably be easier to measure the width of a rib at the point where it folds over the frame and then add on to that width an amount for the corners. The amount of the corners will depend on the width of the folds, but is typically in the range of 6 to 9 mm. From that value it is relatively easy to find the actual front width by extending the length of the pattern as you draw it.

Bellows Folds

Figure 25 shows measurements of the folds. When measuring the folds, first measure the distance (P) along the edge of a pair of "in" and "out" folds including both the ribs and the gaps. Next measure the width of the narrow (N) and wide (W) ribs. Finally, calculate the gap as one-half the difference between the width of the pair and the combined width of the ribs:

This will be easier than attempting to measure the gaps directly. You can verify that the calculated value of the gap is correct in that it should be at least twice the thickness of the cloth.

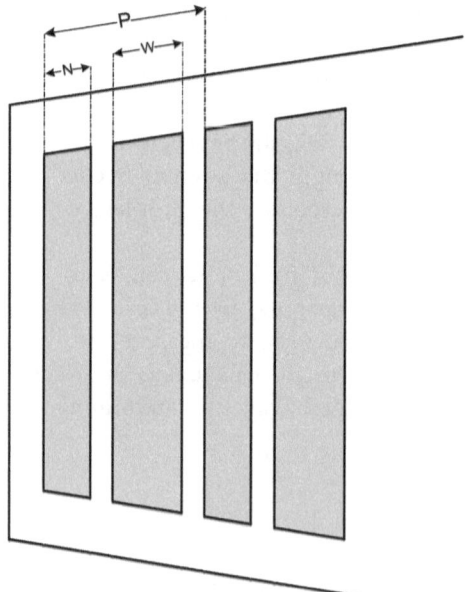

Figure 25 – Measure pairs of stiffeners.

For 6x6 folders the length of a pair of folds will usually be repeated along the length of the bellows. For 6x9 folders the folds will usually narrow at the rear end of the bellows. When you measure pairs along the bellows you may find they vary slightly due to variations during manufacture or because the cloth has become stretched in places. You should measure several pairs to verify the average distance. Typically, the distance of a pair of folds will be in the range of 12 to 15 mm. Typical widths for ribs are 6 to 7 mm for the wide ribs and 4 to 5 mm for the narrow ribs. This yields gaps of 1 to 2 mm.

Once you have determined the width of the folds, sum together the values to get the length of the bellows cloth. This value may not include the flaps at the ends. The length of the flaps can be determined from the amount of space available around the frames, but 5 to 7 mm is typical.

Drawing The Patterns

The next step in constructing the bellows is to draw out the patterns. You can draw the patterns by hand on paper. Optionally, you can use a computer drawing program and then print the patterns using a laser or ink jet printer. The same technique can be used when drawing by hand as on the computer and it is almost as quick. The advantage of using a computer is that you can more easily make small adjustments if you find your initial measurements are slightly off. You can also make multiple copies if you need to make multiple bellows. You do, however, need to use a program that allows you to specify exact dimensions and will print the drawing exactly to scale. Note that some bellows are too large to fit on a standard printer page. You will have to create the template in two sections.

Templates

The first pattern to draw is the basic template for the sections of the bellows. For a square film format you only need one template. For a rectangular format you will need two templates. There is a slight variation depending on whether you have determined the length along the corner or the length along the center.

Begin the template by drawing a horizontal line (AD in Figure 26) equal in length to the width of the bellows at the rear. This length can be either the width at the frame attachment, or can be the actual width at the rear edge.

If you are using the corner length, from each end of the line AD mark a distance equal to one-half the difference between the width of the front and rear (B, C). From these marks, construct two lines perpendicular to the first line (DE, CF) with length equal to the corner length. Lay a ruler down with the start of the ruler at the end of the horizontal line. Swing the ruler over so that the length of the corner on the ruler intersects the vertical line. Alternatively, use a compass set to the length of the corner line to mark the point of intersection. Draw in the corner lines (AE, DF) and then connect the ends of the corners together to form the top line of the trapezoid (EF).

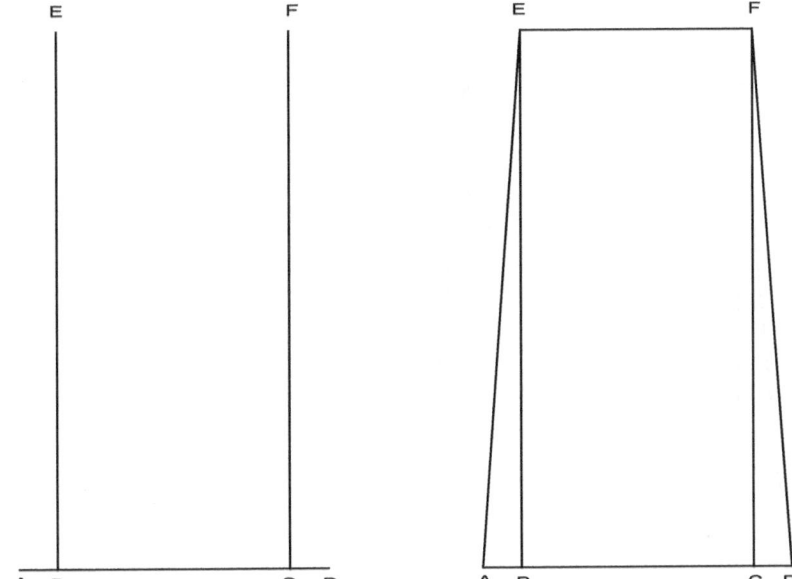

Figure 26 - Drawing the template

If you are using the center length, measure the length of the vertical lines equal to the value you determined for the center length. At the top of the vertical lines, connect the ends of the lines with a horizontal line (EF). Connect the ends of the two horizontal lines to form the corners (AB, DF).

If you are using some value other than the edge of the bellows for the length and width, extend the corner lines to the total length and then connect the ends of the line to form the final pattern (see Figure 27).

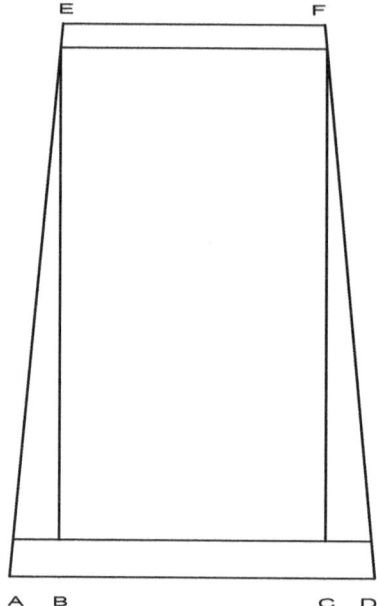

Figure 27 - Extend the corner lines to the total length if needed

Complete pattern

To make a complete pattern, cut out the template that matches the top of the bellows, lay it down on a sheet of paper and carefully mark the four corners. Connect the corners together. Take the template for the sides and lay it down such that the right edge of the template matches the left edge of the section you just drew and again mark the corners and connect them. Repeat this step again on the right edge of the first section to make the three complete sections. Lay the template for the top on each side of the three-section pattern and draw in a half-section on each side. Add a tab of 6-10 mm wide along one side. This tab will form an overlapping seam. Make sure the tab is less than one-half the front width of the outer sections. The final pattern should appear as shown in Figure 28.

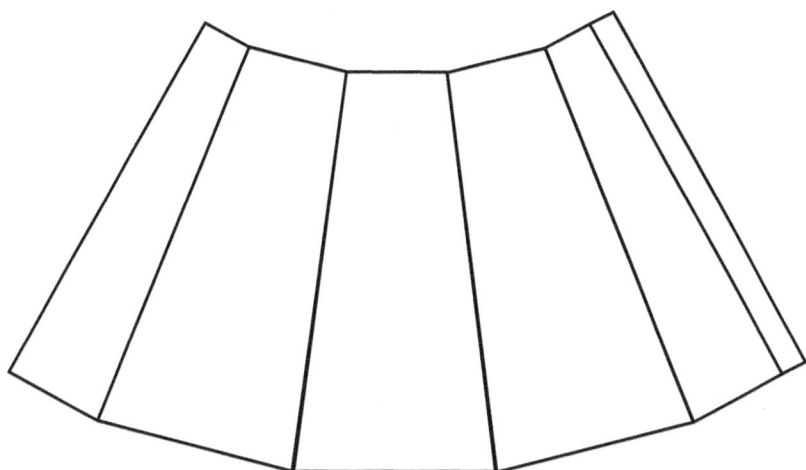

Figure 28 - Complete Pattern – seam in the middle

The seam can also be placed in the corner if the material is thin enough. For a corner seam, duplicate the sides and tops and then add a tab on one of the outer sections.

If you are using a computer drawing program, simply copy the template figures and then rotate each section into position.

Stiffener Rib Pattern

Lay the template down on a piece of rib material and mark the four corners and then connect the corners together. If the first rib is not located at the front edge of the section, measure back along the corner line and mark the starting position. Measure along the corner line marking the position of each rib. Do the same on the opposite corner. Draw horizontal lines between the marks on the corners.

It helps to use a T-square when drawing these lines by hand. Line up the side of the paper using the square. You only need to mark one corner line and then use the T-square to make parallel horizontal lines across each section.

Measure back from the four corners the distance of the cut off of the rib position and make a mark at each position. Draw lines parallel to the corners from front to rear edge to mark the ends of the ribs. You can also draw a line through the center of the section to help in positioning the ribs.

When drawing the stiffeners by hand, it may be better to draw the stiffeners as pairs rather than measuring each strip separately. The steps are shown in Figure 29. First draw the outer lines and setback (1). Next mark horizontal lines at the distance of each stiffener pair (2). Next measure the distance of the first stiffener and draw a horizontal line (3). Measure the gap and draw the next line at (4). Finally measure the gap back from the end of the pair and draw the line at (5). Using this method insures that each pair is the correct length and you are less likely to accumulate small errors along the length of the bellows.

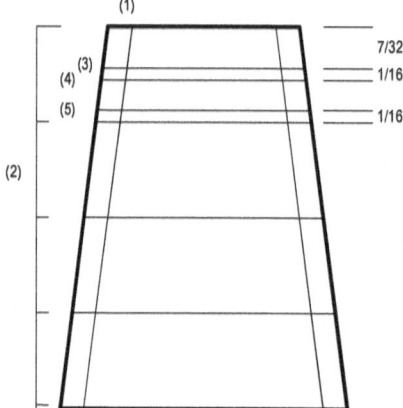

Figure 29 - Drawing stiffeners by marking pairs.

Repeat this for each section of the bellows. Remember that top and bottom sections are the same and side sections are the same, but one pair will begin with a wide strip and the other with a narrow strip.

The following figures show typical stiffener layouts for 6x6 and 6x9 folders. The 6x6 example shows both cut-off stiffeners and pointed stiffeners. You can choose one or the other. The 6x6 example is typical of an AGFA Isolette. The 6x9 example is taken from an AGFA Billy Record. Notice how the width of the stiffeners is less at the rear of the bellows creating for shallower folds that will fit in the small space around the rear frame. These patterns are not exactly to scale. The appendix contains several example patters that are at exact dimensions.

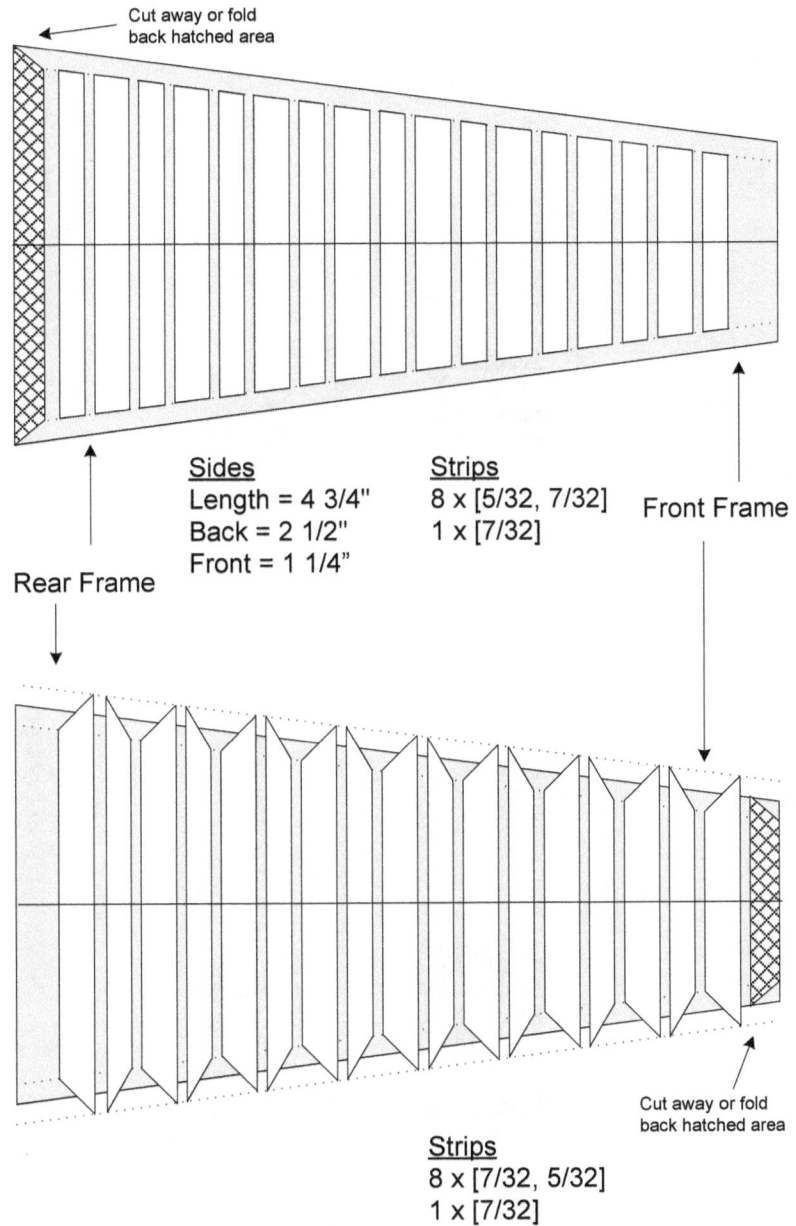

Cut away or fold
back hatched area

Sides
Length = 4 3/4"
Back = 2 1/2"
Front = 1 1/4"

Strips
8 x [5/32, 7/32]
1 x [7/32]

Front Frame

Rear Frame

Cut away or fold
back hatched area

Strips
8 x [7/32, 5/32]
1 x [7/32]

Figure 30 – Typical stiffeners for 6x6 (Isolette)

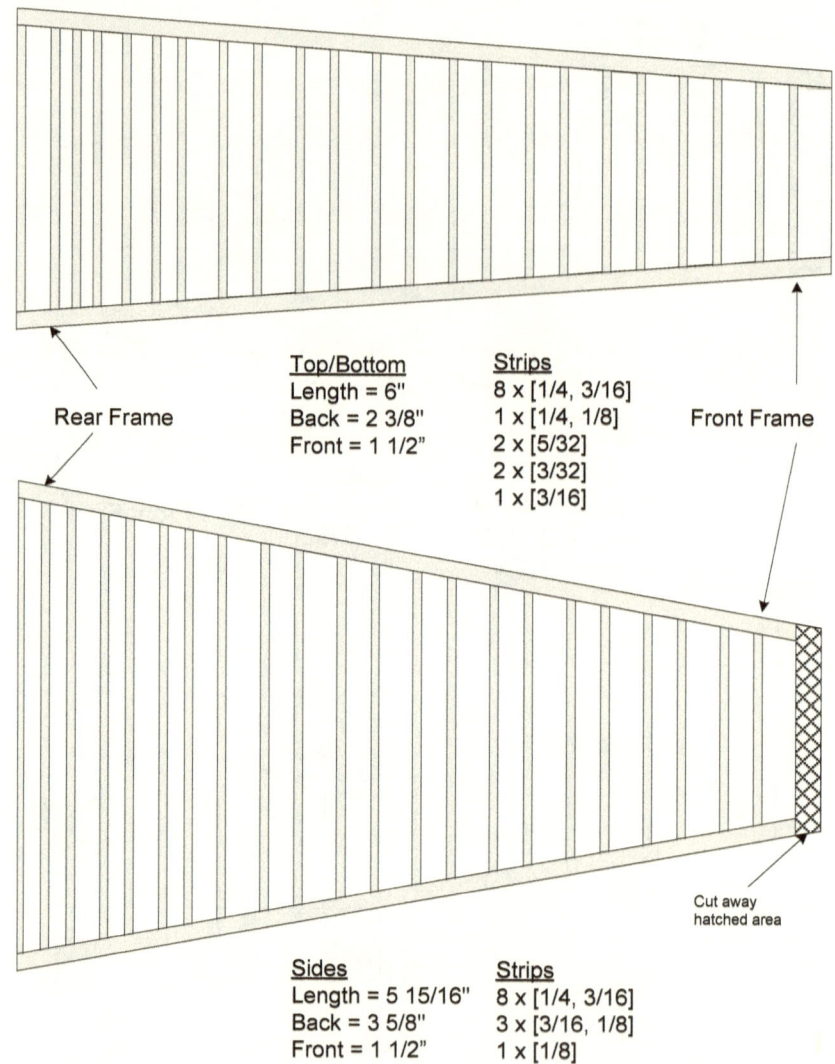

Top/Bottom
Length = 6"
Back = 2 3/8"
Front = 1 1/2"

Strips
8 x [1/4, 3/16]
1 x [1/4, 1/8]
2 x [5/32]
2 x [3/32]
1 x [3/16]

Rear Frame

Front Frame

Cut away
hatched area

Sides
Length = 5 15/16"
Back = 3 5/8"
Front = 1 1/2"

Strips
8 x [1/4, 3/16]
3 x [3/16, 1/8]
1 x [1/8]

Figure 31 – Typical stiffeners for 6x9 (Billy Record)

Making a Form

Using a form helps to keep the bellows straight when folding into a tube. It is possible to make the bellows without the form. However, making the form is not difficult and you should probably use a form to start.

The form can be constructed from poster board, corrugated cardboard, or wood. Balsa wood is a good choice since it is sturdy and can be easily cut with a knife. When using cardboard, fit the pieces together with packaging tape. For wood, use glue or small brads. When using wood, sand off any rough spots on the form and slightly round the corners.

To make the form, use the template(s) you drew for the full pattern to draw panels for the form. On the top and bottom sections, reduce the width by the thickness of the material you use to make the form. Cut two end pieces equal to the width of the bellows at the front and rear.

You may find it helpful to make the form slightly longer than the actual bellows length. This prevents the bellows from sliding off the ends of the form. When measuring the panels, simply extend the corners a small amount on both the front and rear. Adjust the width of the end pieces accordingly.

Figure 32 shows a form made from 3/32" balsa wood. Strips of 1/4" material were added at the corners to give it strength and to give a good surface for gluing.

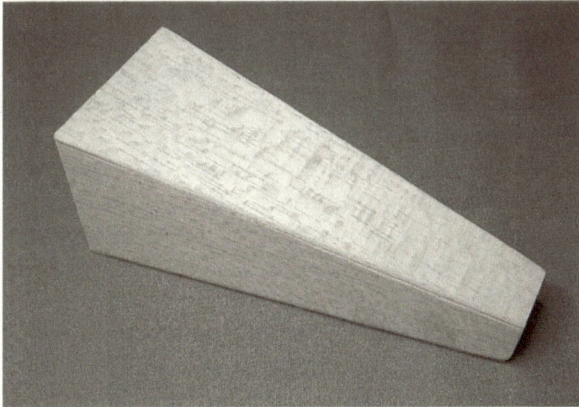

Figure 32 –Bellows form from balsa wood.

55

Assembly of the New Bellows

Once you have the pattern drawn, lay the liner material out with the inside surface down. Lay the pattern onto the liner material and carefully mark the outline of the pattern using a soft lead pencil or fabric marking pencil. Also mark the corners and the center line of each section. These will help as a guide when folding the cloth and positioning the stiffener ribs. Carefully cut the material along the outline.

Lay the covering material out with the outside facing down and then lay the pattern on the material and trace the outline of the bellows pattern. Cut the material along the outline.

If you are using a form, wrap the liner around the form so that the corner lines match the form corners. Use non-permanent tape (such as masking tape) to hold the cloth in position. Spread some contact cement along the cloth where the seam overlaps and then carefully press the edges of the seam together. This is a critical step. If the seam is not straight, the bellows will end up crooked and may interfere with the image path. The contact cement is used to insure the seam does not come apart, but also may not allow you to reposition the cloth once pressed together. If the seam is in the middle the side with the seam will be the top of the bellows. For a corner seam, you make the seam on the top or bottom. If you are not using a form, you can wait to make the seam until the ribs are glued in place.

Cut out a section of the stiffener ribs around the outline but don't cut the ribs apart yet. Lay the rib sheet down on the liner using the center line of the section to position the rib sheet. Mark the position of each rib on the liner material. Cut out each rib and glue it to the liner material using the center mark and the position marks to place each rib. Wait for the glue to dry before proceeding with the cover.

Lay the cover out face down and apply adhesive to the material if needed. Take the cover and carefully position it onto the bellows so that the top of the cover is over the top section of the bellows and is aligned at the front and rear. Wrap the cover around the bellows until you reach the other side. Make sure to smooth out any wrinkles in the cover as you work your way around the bellows. Use contact cement or other adhesive appropriate to your cover material and seal the seam. Carefully cut away any excess material from the cover that overlaps at the front and rear. If needed, set the bellows aside and wait for the cover adhesive to dry.

To make the folds, it is best to place one hand in the rear of the bellows and use the other had on the front. Start folding from the front. Feel along the material to locate the first "out" fold and fold the material down to the inside of the bellows. Pinch the material in the center and work your way out towards the corners making a sharp crease as you go. Stop when you reach the end of the rib. If there is an "in" fold in front, bend the fold back. Rotate the bellows to the next section and again find the first "out" fold. Bend the material along the fold in towards the center of the bellows and pinch it into a crease. Repeat this for the remaining two sections.

Once you have the first fold made, find the end of the next fold and push the material in. Reach inside and pinch the "in" fold together then work your way out towards the corners making a sharp crease in the material. Repeat for the other three sections of the bellows.

Repeat making the out and in folds down the length of the bellows. As you make the folds, push the front of the bellows towards the back to keep the folds in place. As you make the folds, the corners will begin to form automatically. When all the folds are complete pinch each of the corners into a sharp crease to form a triangle.

It is a good idea to leave the bellows folded up for several hours in order to help set the creases. To do this, press the bellows down flat and place it between two pieces of cardboard. Hold the cardboard pieces together with rubber bands or spring clips.

Installing the Bellows

After the creases have set, remove the bellows from the cardboard and insert the front frame into the bellows. You may need to slightly unfold the front of the bellows in order to insert the frame. Optionally, you can insert the frame into the rear of the bellows and work it into position. Make sure the frame is perfectly square to the bellows. If the frame is not square, the bellows will sit crooked in the camera and may interfere with the image path or camera body. Once the frame is in place, use contact cement or glue to attach the front flaps to the frame. If the camera has a rear frame, install the rear frame as well. If necessary, allow the adhesive to dry before installing the bellows in the camera.

Installing the bellows in the camera is the reverse of removal. If the bellows sits in front of the film gate, insert the bellows from the front. Apply adhesive to the rear edge of the bellows and/or the camera frame then press the rear edge of the bellows down into place. If the bellows extends through the film gate, insert the bellows from the rear and carefully work it down into position. Apply adhesive to the rear flaps and press them down into the camera frame. Reinstall the film gate and any screws.

Install the shutter back into the camera. When attaching the shutter retaining ring, be careful not to get the bellows material caught underneath the ring. Sometime is it necessary to slip the ring in place underneath the first fold of the bellows. The fold will usually hold the ring in place while you insert the shutter through the opening in the lens board. Use your fingers or a rubber tool to tighten down the retaining ring until it is finger tight. Use the spanner wrench to make the ring snug.

Once the bellows is in place, make sure the camera will open and close properly. If the camera is not opening properly, look for parts of the bellows that are interfering with the door or struts. If you copied the original bellows properly, it should work smoothly. If you made the bellows too large or the folds too deep, there may not be any other choice but to make the bellows over again. Another possible problem is that you did not get the bellows square to the camera. If there does not seem to be anything interfering with the bellows, it is possible the bellows is just stiff and will work correctly after it has been in use for a while.

Check to make sure the bellows does not interfere with the image path. Open the back of the camera with the bellows extended and set one end of a ruler along the edge of the rear lens. Allow the ruler to lie against the film gate. If the ruler will not lie against the film gate, the folds are extending into the film path and will affect the image.

Finally, check to make sure the bellows is light tight. Take the camera into a dark room and shine a light through the rear opening. There should be no light showing through the bellows. The most likely points of failure are around the front frame and lens opening.

Sample Bellows Patterns

The following pages show some sample bellows patterns. You may photocopy the patterns for personal, non-commercial use. Cut out the pattern around the outer edge and use as a template to make the overall bellows shape. Cut along the inner lines to make the stiffeners. Some of the patterns have a ruler along the side. You can cut that out and use it to mark the stiffener positions or to position the stiffeners by laying the ruler on the cloth.

6x6 Top/Bottom (Generic)

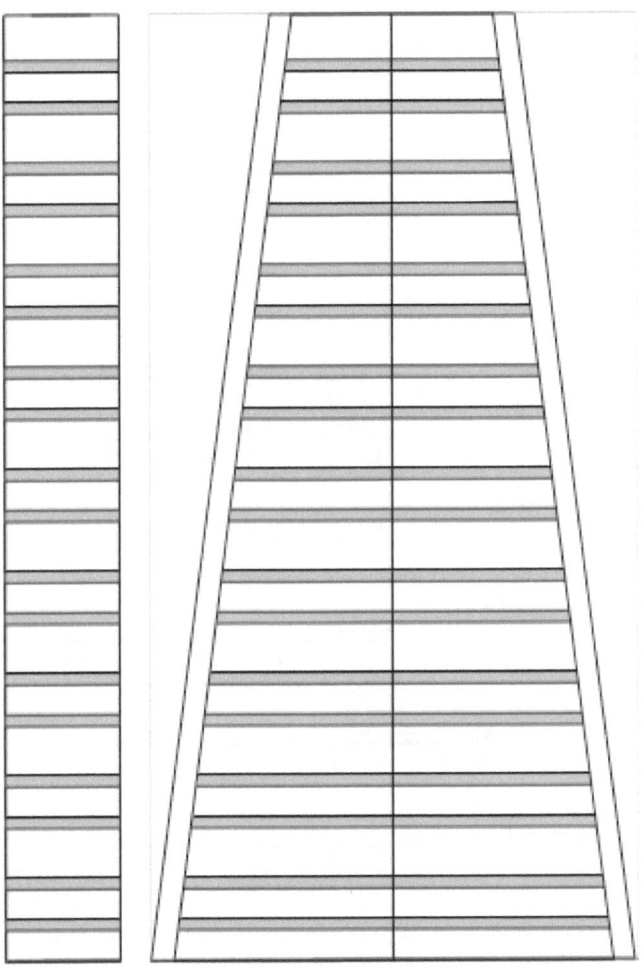

6x6 Sides (Generic)

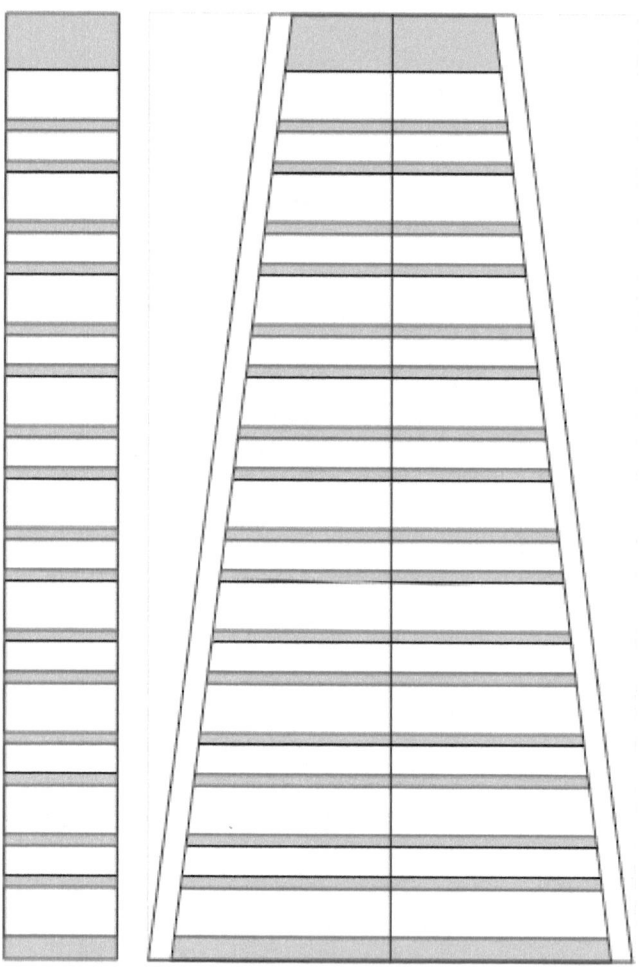

6x9 Top/Bottom (Wirgin Presto)

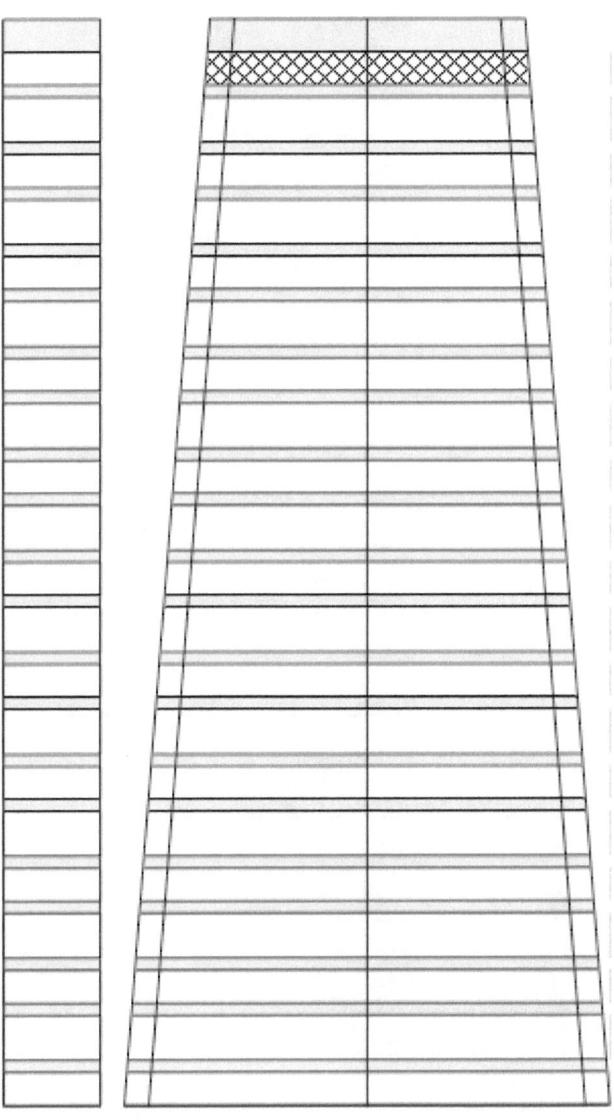

6x9 Sides (Wirgin Presto)

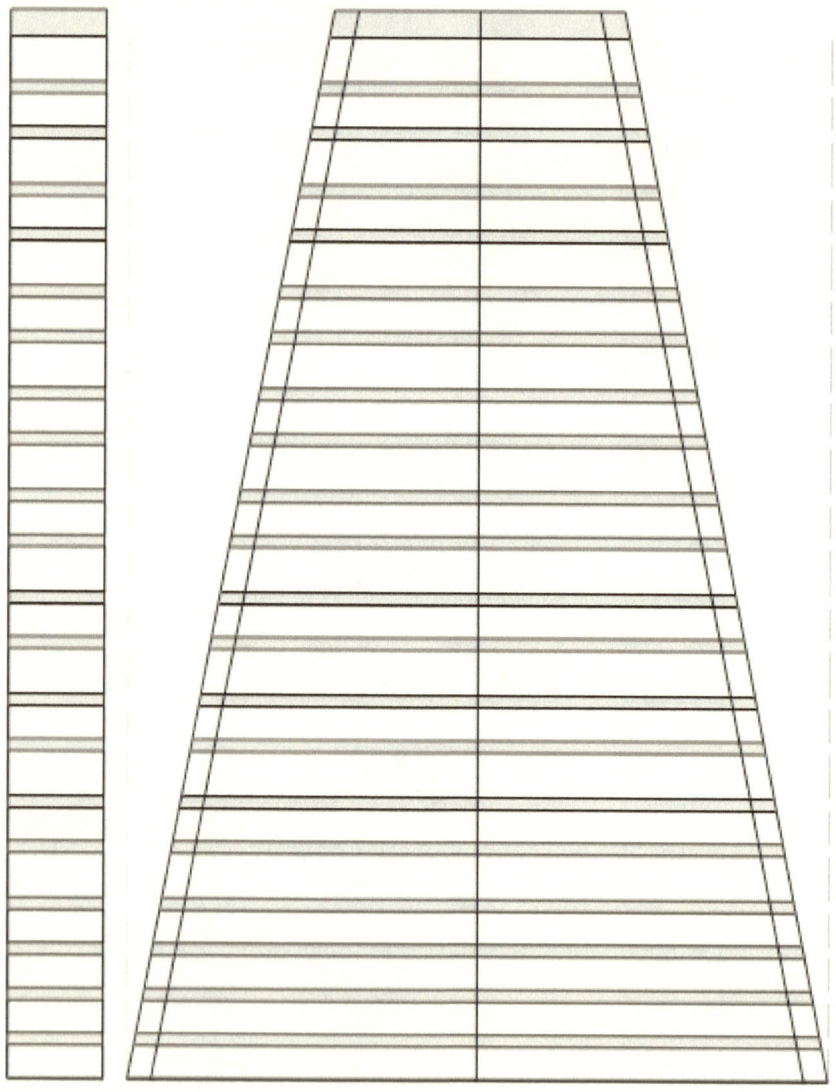

6x9 Sides (Wirgin Auta)

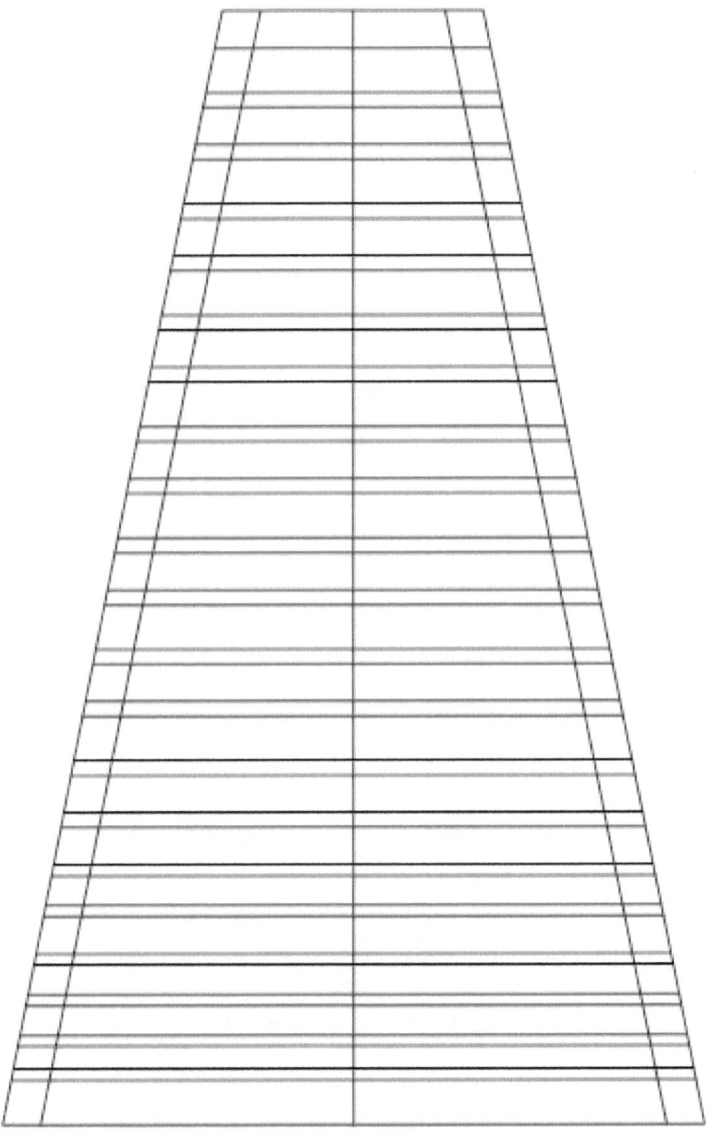

6x9 Top/Bottom (Wirgin Auta)

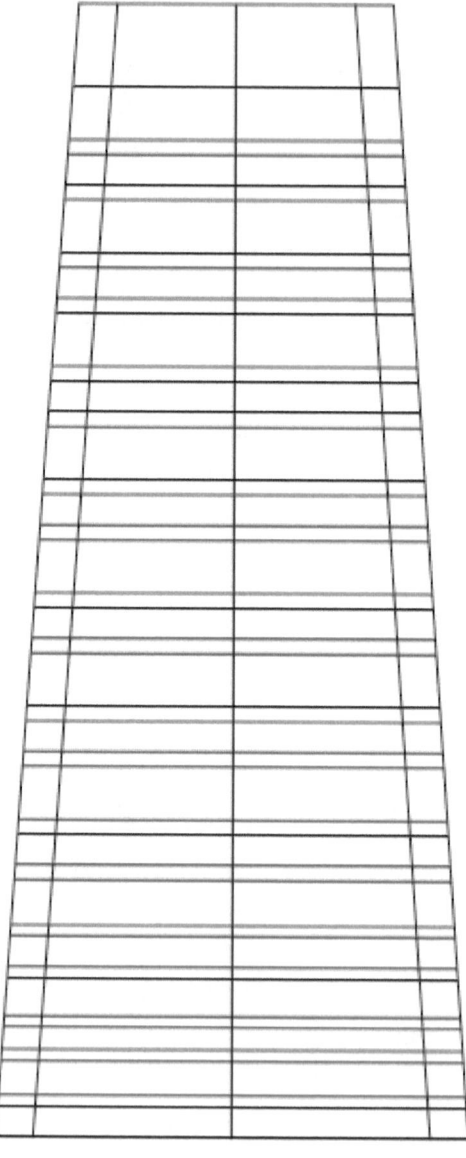

6x9 Sides (Billy Record)

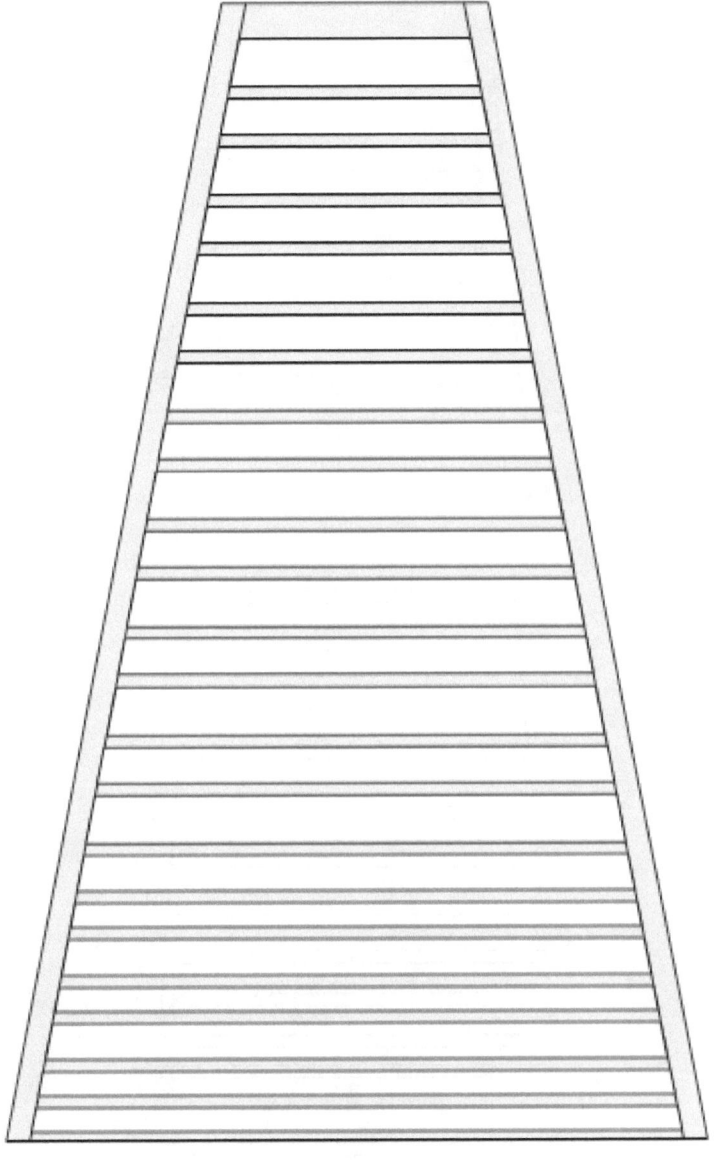

6x9 Top/Bottom (Billy Record)

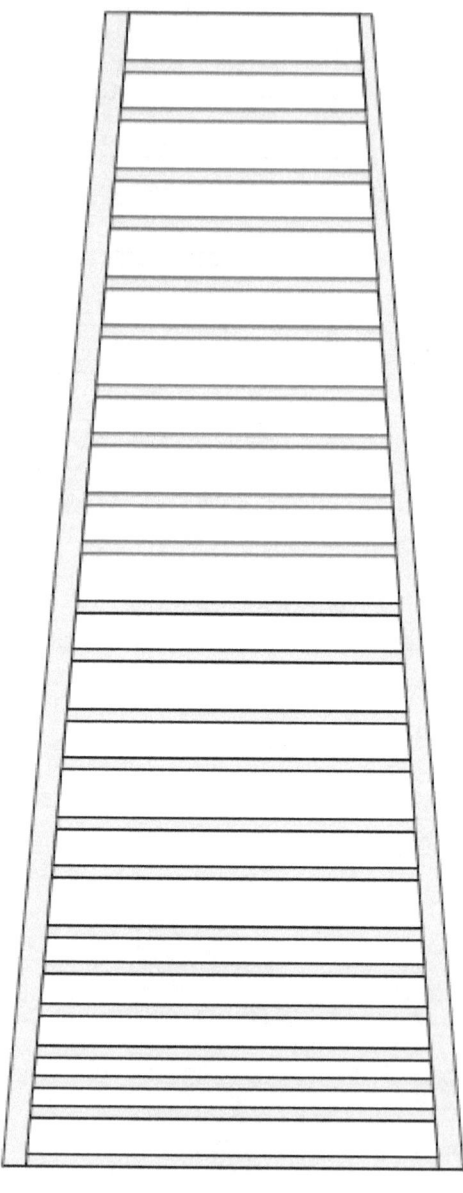

6x9 Sides (No. 1 Kodak Autographic Special)

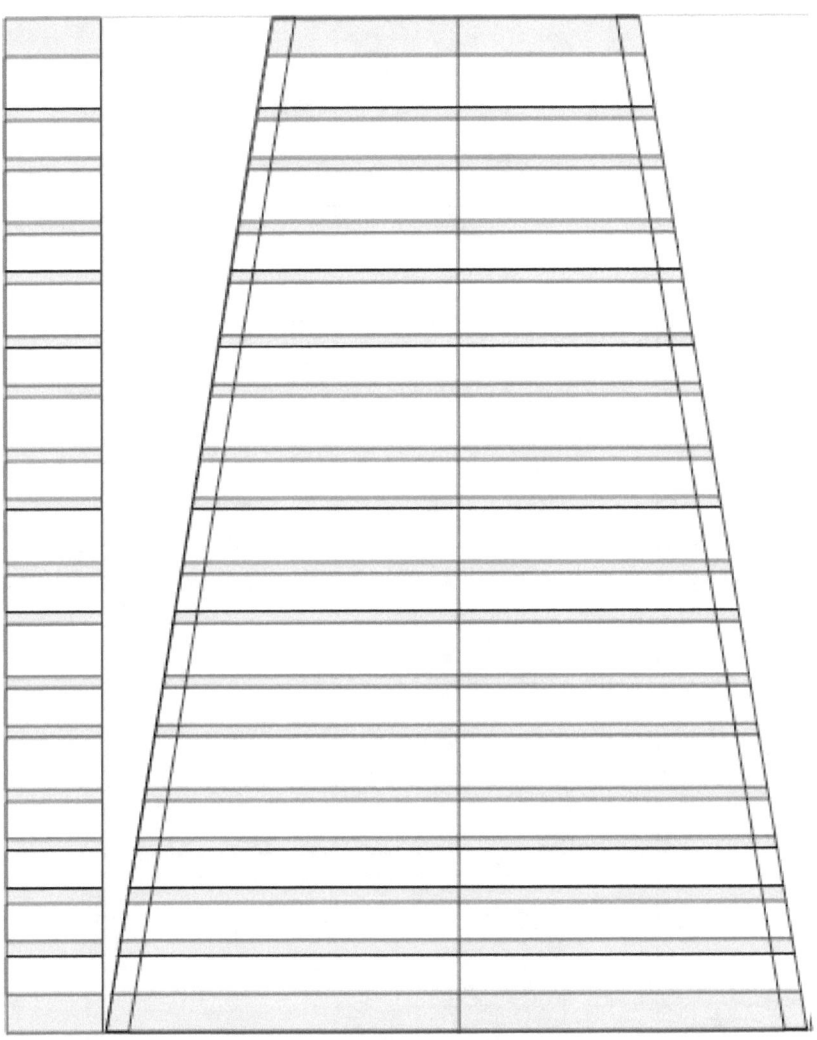

6x9 Top/Bottom (No. 1 Kodak Autographic Special)

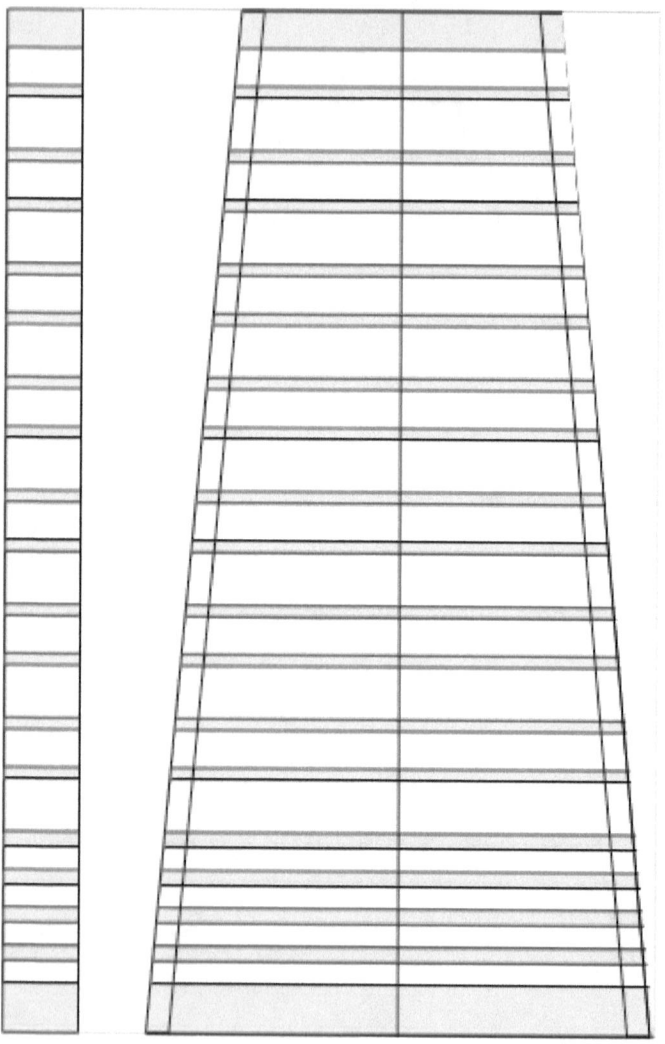